"If you're over fifty and in the dating and flirting world, Flirting After Fifty is the perfect accessory for that classic little black dress. I loved this book!" (Denise Dietz, best selling author of *Beat Up A Cookie*)

Flirting After Fifty
Lessons for grown-up women on how to find love again.

Practical, no-nonsense advice for the midlife woman on how to reclaim her confidence after divorce, widowhood or the loss of love.

- *Flirting "101" - what makes a good flirt?*
- *Starting over - where to begin?*
- *Warning signs of a fortune hunter!*
- *Solutions to awkward dating problems.*
- *Making yourself desirable…and much more…*

Barbara Bellman
Author of **Reaching Women** and **Hitting The Right Nerve**
and
Susan Goldstein, Esq.
Co-author of **The Smart Divorce**

iUniverse, Inc.
New York   Bloomington

Flirting After Fifty
Lessons for grown up women on how to find love again

iUniverse books may be ordered through booksellers or by contacting:

iUniverse
1663 Liberty Drive
Bloomington, IN 47403
www.iuniverse.com
1-800-Authors (1-800-288-4677)

ISBN: 978-0-595-42828-1 (pbk)
ISBN: 978-0-595-71912-9 (cloth)
ISBN: 978-0-595-87166-7 (ebk)

Printed in the United States of America

DEDICATION

This book is dedicated to the women who have the courage, and confidence, to love again – and to all the men who are lucky enough to find them.

Table of Contents

INTRODUCTION

"Friendship's a lot more lasting than love."
"Yeah, but not as entertaining."
Joan Crawford and Jack Carson, actors in *Mildred Pierce*

Who would have thought you'd be alone, and over-50? Whatever your circumstance for being alone at this age, you no doubt realize that meeting someone new is different now. It's confusing at best, and alarming at worst. Can you start over? Should you try? What if you're hurt? Rejected? Will you look foolish? Will you be rebuffed? Is there anyone out there who could love you in your older incarnation?

This is not a book about twirling your hair or batting your eyes. It's not about showing cleavage or playing the coquette. It's about trying to figure out how to be comfortable as a *woman of a certain age* when it comes to the social art of attraction.

There has never been a better time to be a single older woman. We look better, feel more energetic, and are more accomplished and fulfilled. We have more to offer. In short, we're pretty good company.

We're grown-ups who have lived interesting lives. Some of us have had careers, raised families, and contributed time and resources to numerous worthy causes. We've created, and planned, and grown. And we are worthy! But how do we find someone who recognizes us for the person we have become rather than seeing only the toll age and work has taken on our bodies? Where to start? What to say? Who could have predicted it would be this way?

There is an old proverb that says, *"No road is long with good company."*

We are living longer than previous generations. And so are the men. Sharing the journey can be so much more interesting than going forward alone.

Is flirting for everyone? Maybe not. But for those who want to be in love again, here are stories, experiences, and insights to inspire and motivate you to expand your comfort zone and take a chance again.

We've met hundreds of women whose hearts still want to beat to the tune of a new romance. They haven't given up, but have lost the way. Frightened to make a new mistake or repeat an old one, their confidence has waned with the passing years and the idea of being an *object of desire* feels foolish and unrealistic. But it doesn't have to be.

We each have careers in which we work with men and women in marketing and legal services. In our respective fields, we have needed to observe behavior in order to understand what works, what doesn't, and why. Though we each see life through different professional lenses, it's our business to observe and then use those observations.

We are both over 50. We approached this subject out of curiosity and a desire to figure out why some people are better able to connect than others and how some otherwise good catches never got caught, while others have someone on the line all the time.

There was much to learn. As friends and successful authors we agreed to join each other in this discovery and thus began our collaboration to interview women about their experiences and insights.

Dozens of women shared their stories of hope, regret, embarrassment, rejection, and love. We heard about the good, the sad and the funny. We didn't have all the answers, but we had a lot of questions and wanted to explore how women can improve their chances at attracting the opposite sex through the lost (or forgotten) art of flirtation.

Regardless of a woman's age, love is a frequent topic of conversation. Relationships are everywhere we turn in the books we read, the movies we watch, daytime and nighttime television and in the questions we ask on a daily basis: *Has she met someone? Is she dating? Did she think he was attractive? Is he available? Does she want to meet someone? Did he leave her for someone?*

The interest, curiosity, spark, desire or need – call it what you will – doesn't end at the age of fifty or thereafter. To the contrary. That's when it gets really interesting. If you're in that demographic defined as *50-plus*, you may think you're relegated to the status of *second class citizen*, as if a slightly slower walk, quieter music, and a little gray should keep you down. Certainly you need to brace yourself for obstacles that didn't exist in your younger dating years. But obstacles are often easily pushed, shoved or kicked away. Read on.

Many women retreat at the thought of finding a new relationship because they fear rejection, failure or vulnerability. What we've learned, however, is that all women, regardless of age, can jump-start their confidence, have fun and start over. They can feel the tingle and the heat and know it's not just hot flashes! They've learned that this part of their lives isn't over; it's just beginning to unfold anew as it can for you.

We've heard endless complaints from women who lament their inability to meet the right someone. They mask their insecurities by making excuses: *"Men are creeps. The good ones are taken. He's too old, fat, bald, fussy, sickly, boring."* Sound familiar?

Or they self-deprecate: "Why would he want me? I'm too old, fat, wrinkly, fussy, sickly, and boring." Is that you? Perhaps it's time to re-think your point of view.

It's easy to make excuses, hide and withdraw. It's risky to take a chance to be vulnerable again – to rebuild confidence buried under the layers of past disappointments, or just the normal atrophy of being out of practice and realizing that the game has changed since you last played it. But here's the thing: why shouldn't the years going forward be lived fully and happily? If you want to meet someone with whom to share your journey, this book will inspire you to consider the possibilities.

Being a good flirt is about confidence. Your skin may not fit as tightly as it did thirty years ago, nor is your hair as abundant. Your face probably has a few lines and your heart, by now, has a few scars. A look in the mirror can be disheartening as the impulse to compare the stranger in the mirror to the *younger you* is unavoidable. But stop staring at the old image and create a new one. And flirting is a great place to start.

Flirting is the adult version of playing. It's about expressing interest in someone else through a variety of age-appropriate ways without demanding a particular outcome to validate the moment. It's about having fun. Just as everyone is not an appropriate playmate for a child, not everyone is a good candidate for flirting. With your increased maturity also comes the responsibility of using judgment and making good decisions about where and with whom you will play.

Flirting is a state of mind, born of a sense of self that accepts and likes who you are, and who you are to others.

This book offers insight and understanding to women who have discovered it's a new and unfamiliar game out there, and want to learn new ways to play it.

Our hope is that you will be inspired to re-enter the world of flirting. Your life isn't over at 50. It's a new stage and how we play it in the next half of our lives is ours to create. There's no reason to have a different attitude at 60 than at 16. As Frank Sinatra crooned: *"Here is the best part. You have a head start, if you are among the very young at heart."*

Chapter 1
THE PARTY ISN'T OVER, IT'S JUST BEGINNING

"Love doesn't make the world go 'round.
Love is what makes the ride worthwhile."
Franklin P. Jones, *author*

"I love that you get cold when it is 71 degrees out.
I love that it takes you an hour and a half to order a sandwich.
I love that you get 'a little crinkle above your nose when you're looking at me
like I'm nuts. I love that after I spend a day with you, I can still smell your
perfume on my clothes. And I love that you're the last person I want to talk
to before I go to sleep at night. And it's not because I'm lonely, and it's not
because it's New Year's Eve. I came here tonight because when you realize
you want to spend the rest of your life with somebody, you want the rest of
your life to start as soon as possible."
Billy Crystal to Meg Ryan in *When Harry Met Sally*

Did you just catch your breath or get a wee bit teary or feel your heart
pound a little faster? With all the romantic movies of the past ninety years,
for many of us, these words resonate more than most. Why? Could it be
because with all the hoopla about love – love is in the small details? We want
to be loved for who we are. We need to love him for who he is. And isn't it
just the most wondrous and remarkable thing when who you are and who he
is feels right for both of you? But it can't happen unless you're willing to clear
away the cobwebs and make room for the real thing to come along.

Often, while we wait and wonder if love will ever find us, we fill our time
with clutter, and waste time in relationships that will go nowhere. No doubt,

1

it's important to be active and productive, not sit home waiting for the phone to ring. Our lives can and should be filled with more than a longing for love. And while you certainly are capable of going it alone quite nicely, is that your only choice? Your best choice? To open your heart to love, you have to make room for it to happen.

What's going on?

- Middle-age sex is now a permanent fixture in our popular culture, whether it is in movies, novels, television or watching sixty-year-old rock 'n roll stars revving it up on stage to the squeals of women of all ages. Our generation is more vital, sexual, and energetic than any previous generation.

- Gyms have low impact classes for boomers to shape up so that they can ship out to new frontiers. We have grown up with health and fitness being a part of our lives. We're organic, natural, involved in our image and want to stay healthy.

- The Internet has provided us with new, pain-free ways to test the *singles' waters*, one baby boomer step at a time. Go to singles sites and see how many *50-plus* men await you. Even if you're not yet comfortable getting out there for a face to face, check it out. It's comforting to know there actually are a lot of men out there looking for love, too.

- Universities, extension classes, and vocational facilities welcome the more experienced, mature student who wants to embellish an education, train for something new or simply learn about a new topic. Lifelong growth means keeping your mind alive and interesting. And *everyone* is more *interested* in interesting people.

- If you can't face the mirror, consider this: Never have we lived in a time when modern medicine can do more to firm up, de-wrinkle, enhance or subtract. Products, techniques, procedures, and programs abound that can help us look and feel younger than our years.

- Viagra, hormones, and various medications have made the prospect of a continued sex life a reality. Our tolerance for, and awareness of a little assistance here and there makes the variety and frequency of our love making more interesting. We are now less insecure, inhibited, and immature, and can openly admit to wanting, needing, and having sex without apologies to our parents, our kids, or our friends.

- The covers of magazines feature beautiful *over-50* women who look fabulous with their gray hair and fine lines. It's no longer necessary to hide our age. In fact, as we continue to dominate the media, the markets, and the mindsets of our world with our vast numbers and purchasing power, *older* is not only *wiser*, but also more beautiful.

If you find you want to meet someone, you can now flirt, armed with the experience acquired over half a century and a chance for a *do-over* in the decades to follow. Though there are some newer challenges and the prospect of encountering occasional awkward moments, *mature* flirting has some *distinct advantages*.

Such as:

- You can now be both sexy and smart.
- You have a better idea who your ideal mate should be.
- You are more established, with a foundation of home and job to give you a secure base.
- You have a network of friends and family with whom to share both good and bad.
- You have a better, more mature understanding of the world.
- You have a clearer perspective of what you want and need.
- You understand life's bumpy path.
- You have the confidence that comes with age and experience.

We all change as we age. Many of us know that we can take steps to stem the tide of these changes: Working out, coloring our hair (or not), modifying our clothing to better flatter our changing figures, adjusting our makeup to suit our skin and coloring, perhaps getting a few nips and tucks if we so decide. Others of us accept the gray, the extra pounds and the lines that say *we've been there.*

Regardless of your path, the new you in the mirror has the same soul as before. And while you've changed, so have the men. Though they look older too, many still have a lively sparkle in their eyes. Be prepared to see beyond the balding head, lined face or distinct paunch when a man casts an interested look in your direction. Behind the mileage of age, there may be someone who could keep you smiling for the next forty years.

We continue to re-define the definitions and expectations of what it is to age as we declare that *50 is the new 40.* Mature women are world leaders, famous authors, brilliant doctors, and trail blazers. The average age for active adventure travel is 55 and no, we aren't sitting on the bus, the rocker, or our laurels. We are more alive than any generation preceding us, and we are positive role models for future generations.

In short, we're a long way from drafting the epitaphs for our headstones.

But a little caution goes a long way.

Flirting well is a function of confidence, and the goal is to encourage you to find all the ways you can to cultivate an improved sense of self. Friends and family want you to *pick yourself up, dust yourself off and get back in the game* because they want to see you happy and complete. That's why they will invite you to all kinds of outings where you can see and be seen.

Occasions of any sort (weddings, funerals, and graduations) are great places to meet new people. So are parties, dinners, and sports events. But flirt with someone else's man and you will find those invitations dwindle – or else find yourself seated at the graveyard table with other single women, close to the kitchen. Don't threaten the turf of married (or involved) women by inadvertently or overtly flirting with their men. You can be charming without being predatory. If you are too provocative, the men will surely look at you, but their women will look at them and steer them away; a sure way to put an end to future invitations.

A happy ending is a good place to start.

Meredith's Story

59 year old Meredith had given up on finding love when she reluctantly agreed to attend the wedding of a young co-worker. Faced with the choice of being conservatively dressed or tastefully showing a little cleavage, she agonized over how she would be perceived and explained her dilemma to the bride. Reassured that she would be seated with people who would not be threatened by her more festive gown, she was determined to have a good time at the wedding, albeit without a partner. Her attitude, attire, and outlook helped her overcome any concerns of being alone.

At the reception following the ceremony, she was seated at a table comprised of friendly and welcoming couples and singles. Conversation was lively and they danced and laughed throughout the evening. Meredith didn't feel unwelcome, out of place, or judged. During the dinner, one of the guests turned to her, and, motioning toward her date said, "you know, we aren't really together, together." A few minutes later, that date asked Meredith to dance. Out of courtesy, Meredith politely asked permission from his lady, who quickly nodded her approval, and off they went. On the floor they danced just once, but the electricity between them was intense. Though they lived in opposite parts of the country he wanted her number.

"I want to get to know you," he said. *"But I'm geographically undesirable!"* she exclaimed. *"I can travel,"* he countered. *"I'll give you my number,"* she smiled. *And he quickly committed it to memory.*

The following Monday, he called at 8 A.M. "Hello gorgeous!" he began. *And they were off!*

Neither of them expected the magic to happen. Certainly not Meredith. But it did. It wasn't fantasy, though it was fantastic. Nor fiction, though it seemed too good to be true. And the magicians behind the *trick* turned out to be the bride and groom, who had planned the table seating with this outcome in mind!

The moral of the tale is that love can happen unusually, unexpectedly and very quickly. But you have to be ready to answer its call, or its whistle. You know how to whistle, don't you?

Chapter 2
YOU KNOW YOU'RE READY WHEN...

"To fear love is to fear life and those who fear life
are already three parts dead."
Bertrand Russell, *British philosopher, author*

Flirting makes a statement. It says you're confident, you feel good about yourself, and good about the person with whom you are flirting. But it goes further than that. It says you're ready, if not for love, then for the next best thing – the pursuit of it.

When do you know you're ready to flirt, to date, to get back into the game? One thought is, you know you're ready when your desire for love is greater than your fear of being hurt by it. It's possible you weren't ready a moment sooner, but maybe not. Maybe you were just too scared to face it.

What of the yearning to *be* loved? We know we have to be in a position to open our hearts, to be vulnerable, to be willing to risk being exposed, foolish or rejected in order to be receptive to love. It's that vulnerability that makes us approachable, likeable and ultimately desirable. But that vulnerable spot is a scary place; it's a nerve that is raw and exposed.

"Love is an irresistible desire to be irresistibly desired."
(Robert Frost, *poet*)

Too many women sulk around like the *walking wounded*. They carry around their ended love affairs or lost loves as if they've grown some monstrous second head, reminding them of past hurts, stupid mistakes, and bad decisions. They remember the pain of being rebuffed, having the fires of their affection snuffed as they were left to their own devices to cope with healing. If widowed, friends and family are supportive, for a while. If divorced, friends and family lend some support but often it's accompanied with a cheerleader-like chant of *move on* and *it's time to get over it*. Again, we are ultimately left to mend alone as mending, as we quickly learn, is a seriously solitary endeavor.

For many of us, healing is never really complete, and leaves us wary and overly cautious about falling victim to new assaults and pain. The older we get, the more blows we've endured, and the less willing we are to tread the love minefield again. Some of us learn to become comfortable with being alone and justify that aloneness by enjoying our space, relishing the uncomplicated nature of our private time and justify our life by saying that we are just too set in our ways.

Others go from short-term relationships, to long distance liaisons, to occasional flings or weekend romances, content to be sustained by such brief encounters. These little samples keep them briefly satisfied, and unencumbered. Some women are fine with things as things are; they're not really looking for anything permanent.

There are those who don't want any relationship at all, but enjoy occasional recreational sex and an abundance of friendships for movies, parties, and dinners, communicating to every friend that sooner or later there's an expiration date to the connection.

"Love is the answer, but while you're waiting for the answer, sex raises some pretty good questions." (Woody Allen, *author, director, actor*)

Some women are so eager to prove they can live alone quite nicely, thank you, that they miss a good thing when it comes along. Being single and alone can be great. You can be quite content. Most of all, you are safe. But if you have any interest in coupling again, and can open yourself to the possibility of someone sharing your life, your bed, your closet, and your heart, you must be ready to flirt in earnest and it can't all be on your terms. *"Too old to change,"* you say? Too stuck in your ways? OK. Maybe you are. In which case, this advice won't be of much value to you. But if you are ready to give *change* a chance, the adventure may be well worth getting out of your comfort zone.

One woman we spoke with went through a withering divorce. Her husband had done a convincing job telling her she was ugly, stupid and that no one would ever, ever want her again. She became timid, depressed, and lonely. Though her friends encouraged her to try to meet someone else, she could not shake her insecurity and poor self-image. Her former husband had successfully embedded those negative feelings into her psyche and she was stuck in being miserable.

One day her best friend said, *"Unless you make some effort to pull out of this funk, I will never speak to you again. I insist you go online, and go out on at least 3 dates."* When her friend actually stopped speaking to her she signed up for a dating service. The outcome? She met a great guy. It took a while, but for her friend's insistence, it wouldn't have happened at all. Do you need that kind of kick to give you courage?

"Love is life. And, if you miss love, you miss life."
(Leo Buscaglia, PhD, *author, professor, lecturer*)

It takes courage to love. It's unsettling to feel oneself being pulled toward another. At this age it's unexpected. It's unfamiliar. It disturbs the equilibrium. It's the unknown and we are less receptive to trying new things (or people). To behave out of character or put ourselves in a different setting throws us off center. The older we get, the more we remember how we have been hurt by love, or the loss of it. For many, that fear is just too great and the need to insulate from such intense feelings may cloud any opportunity for being authentic and trusting, and willing to make accommodations for another. The comfort we have in doing the same things the same way with the same people may make us feel secure. *But it's also a rut.* When did we ever think being stuck in a rut was good? Change is both inevitable and necessary to grow.

"Love is everything it's cracked up to be. That's why people are cynical about it. It really is worth fighting for, being brave for, risking everything for. And the trouble is, if you don't risk anything, you risk even more."
(Erica Jong, *author*)

We lose people we love to death, estrangement, tragedy or the natural course of life itself. But when it comes to matters of the heart, we have choices. Choosing to feel, to be open to love no matter its risk, is to embrace all the best life has to offer. Yes, we can learn to enjoy our alone time and live completely satisfying lives without a love interest. But the journey may be richer and more fun with someone – the right one – to share it. It is to that spirit of adventure, daring, and enthusiasm for the possibility of love that we say, go flirt. You've got nothing to lose but your heart.

Chapter 3
LOVE ISN'T BLIND

"The average man is more interested in a woman who is interested in him than he is in a woman with beautiful legs."
George Sand, *author*

There are a lot of myths that diminish our confidence, but let's discuss the one that really needs to be tackled and quashed. It's the one that says we're old, and therefore less desirable.

If ever there was a myth-busting event, it was the marriage of Camilla Parker Bowles to Prince Charles. He once had Diana, and he could have any number of younger women, but the woman who won his heart was Camilla; not only an over-50 woman, but a woman older than he is! She may have lacked the glamour of Diana, and the allure of her youth, but whatever Camilla had, he was willing to forsake all to have her in his life and by his side. Love isn't blind. It sees what it wants and finds beauty where it chooses.

Apparently Camilla didn't get the memo that said:
- Men only want younger women.
- Men only want beautiful women.
- Men only want women who make them look good.
- Men only want women who are a size 6 or smaller.
- Men don't look at women with crow's feet, cellulite and age spots.
- Men don't want used goods.

From coast to coast, we hear these comments again and again. Yet there are older women who have turned a deaf ear to these clichés, and move forward with confidence and enthusiasm. For them, love and romance is ageless.

Why then, do these negative thoughts churn non-stop in the minds of so many *50-plus singles?*

For starters, we see examples all the time of some middle-aged men trying to hang onto their own fleeting youth by sporting younger women on their arms. It does happen, especially in celebrity and moneyed circles. The power of his position is attractive to a woman, any woman. And many times these men think, *why not?* But at what price does a man choose a *trophy* over a woman more his age? Will she ultimately make him feel older or younger? Her pace is faster, her memory is sharper and sexually, well, he may actually require chemicals to perform. Will he worry that she will tire of him, stray, or want him only for his money? A trophy can tarnish fast.

In glitzy cities such as Los Angeles and Las Vegas, where appreciation for the outer shell rather than the inner person resonates more noticeably, men are guiltier of "trophy-ism". To some extent, this obsession with youth is regional, and more informed by lifestyle. Where intelligence, worldliness, sensuality and "perspective" are values, men want a more mature woman, not a toy.

Across the country, and indeed, in most cultures throughout the world, older women are considered seasoned, passionate, deep, caring, and even more important, *interesting!* A woman who can sustain a good conversation, laugh from the gut, demonstrate a willingness to explore, show a tolerance for life's many curve balls and still manage to not take herself too seriously, is a more desirable companion than a vapid ingénue obsessed with her looks, clothes, or the names of the latest chic restaurants.

This isn't to say that all young women are shallow. They're not. But closer observation shows that most men aren't nearly as superficial as they are often accused of being. In fact, many run a lot deeper, *and a lot hotter* than we often give them credit for and they prefer a woman with whom they can relate, rather than work to impress.

Once the fever of sex begins to cool, men want women in their lives with whom they can talk and laugh; women who understand them and their needs. Younger, thinner, and tighter may make for enticing appetizers, but such are rarely satisfying as the main course.

Like heat-seeking missiles, men gravitate to an energy source that nurtures and thrills in both familiar and unexpected ways: Familiar, in that the energy provides comfort, safety, and stimulation. Unexpected, in that sometimes the energy takes them places they haven't been before and, perhaps with trepidation, still want to go. Often, the source of that energy is packaged differently from what they might have initially thought appealing. But as we all adjust our expectations, we're obliged to revise our views of attraction. It's nature's way of keeping us in the game.

As we age, our notion of what is desirable changes. Yes, we can still admire young beauty, but we don't have to pursue it. Many people we talked with agreed that a firm belly and tight behind is appealing, but a little girth isn't necessarily a turn-off. Ditto gray hair or a baldhead. Our maturity allows us to see beyond the superficial, and believe it or not, men can do that too. And for the ones who can't, take a pass on those guys. Really, would you desire a man who is so narcissistic he preferred arm candy instead of you?

Confident, secure men want confident, secure women. And that often comes with age. We know it and men know it too.

Being fully alive means having diverse interests, being curious about the world, learning new things, having a sense of adventure, going to new and different places, and, of course, being open to meeting new people. It invigorates us. And those who nurture that energy enjoy more out of life. Isn't it more life-affirming to look forward to what's next, rather than look back with longing for the past? Why should we regret roads not taken that are still there, ready for the walk?

The clock doesn't wind backwards, so it's best to come to terms with your old attributes and start looking forward. You can take to your bed, or come to grips with reality and cultivate new, compelling, fascinating, and wonderful qualities.

Remember that as long as your flame has not extinguished, you can still kindle an energy from within that will light up a room when you enter.

"We must always have old memories and young hopes."
(Arsene Houssaye, *author, poet*)

A secure and happy older woman once said that the secret to happiness is having someone to love, something to do, and something to look forward to; all things we can control, if we choose.

Too often women fear the future and pull in the corners of their world, fueled with excuses: *"I can't sleep in a strange bed. I'm used to waking up in my home. I have my routines. I can't deal with jet lag."* They don't go out at night because of more excuses. *"I can't see to drive and I don't want to go alone."* They don't experiment with different restaurants because they can't eat this or that, they're used to the same old place, or it's too far to drive. They don't use a computer because they're *too old to learn*. No text messaging because it's too complicated. They don't learn anything new because they think they're too old, it's too hard, it's not important. Excuses, excuses, excuses!

People like this, and we all know them, *are boring*. It's why their children don't visit often, or why friends stop calling. It's why they are seen walking their dogs alone, and grouse about how the world has gone wrong. They become malcontents, angry that their lives aren't more interesting. *"I can't, I won't, I shouldn't"* is their automatic response when confronted with new possibilities. They refuse to embrace life.

But embracing life is what it takes to meet someone new. It is precisely the embracing of life, *a new life*, which makes flirting more than something nice to do. It's a lifesaver.

"A man is not old until regrets take the place of dreams."
(John Barrymore, *actor*)

Consider those people whom, at any age, are delightful company. We like to talk to them and do things with and for them. They are always invited to parties because they chip in, mingle, and bring their *party faces* and personalities. They introduce themselves to other people and tend to draw others out. They don't reluctantly enter a room, find a quiet corner and wait for someone to entertain them. In a nutshell, they know how to have fun, how to like others and be liked.

We've all walked into a room full of strangers and within minutes it's clear who the life of the party is. It's not that the person is better looking, or loudest or funniest. Rather, it is that person who compels us, who draws us into his or her energy field like a magnet.

What makes people like that so sought after? They are the ones who smile, who have a kind word, who are confident, and unafraid. They are friendly and open and eager to talk about what they're doing, and interested, genuinely, in what you are doing. They don't start and stop every conversation with what they like or what they don't. They focus on others, gently drawing them out with sincere interest. None of this non-stop talk about cholesterol levels, heart disease, tumors, arthritis, and all the toils of aging. They may be creaking but they don't need to share every ache and pain. Their zest and enthusiasm for others is an inspiration and is sometimes contagious. They make us feel good and we follow by example.

Judi's Story
Judi was a perfect example of someone for whom life was one big adventure. Un-self conscious in the extreme, she decided to have a singles-only holiday party as a way to expand her social network and jump-start the holiday season. She

came up with an interesting and unusual gimmick for an icebreaker. On the night of her party when people started arriving, they walked in to find the table wasn't set, hors d'oeurves were still in the fridge, and no drinks were out for guests. Was it the wrong night? Why wasn't everything ready for company? Contrary to conventional wisdom, Judi planned not to be ready. One by one, as her guests arrived, they realized the party needed some organization, and before they knew it, they were conscripted into service. Though they arrived as strangers, the need to get the party going gave them an excuse to do something purposeful and engage in a task together. A common goal incited conversation and activity and because each person had something to do, the focus was on the job at hand, not on waiting around feeling awkward until the wine kicked in. The party turned strangers into teammates, and cleverly bypassed all the awkwardness of initial small talk.

"Work like you don't need the money. Love like you've never been hurt. Dance like nobody's watching." (Satchel Paige, *American athlete*)

OK. Not everyone is as bold as Judi. You're not going to suddenly transform into someone you're not. But to move the ball forward, you have to move, even if it's in dribbles.

Nancy's Story

Take Nancy, for instance. By day, she is a powerful lady, the CEO of a company that employs 300 people. She is decisive, analytical, and strong. But when it comes to connecting with anyone on a personal level, she retreats into a carefully constructed cocoon of efficiency, distance and self-control though she would love for it to be otherwise. Nancy wants to meet the right man but when attending a party, she lingers to the side, trying to look at ease, while inwardly she is terrified. She asked what she could do to find a comfort level in social situations and make herself more appealing to men. Viewing it as a challenge, similar to any other she might face in her business world, we scripted her to try some different approaches.

We suggested she:

- Check out the room and select a person she'd like to meet.
- Give some thought to a good opening line (see our Chapter: Flirting Fire Starters) that fits her comfort level, the look of the person she wants to meet, and the situation.
- Be truthful. Start her conversation by admitting she is usually shy, but that there is something about him that motivated her to overcome it and start a conversation.

Because Nancy is accustomed to assuming the right facade for the role she needs to play, this mini-script helped her formulate a game plan that worked to get her over the hurdle of making the approach.

Every experience is a form of practice. If one guy isn't it, maybe the next one will be. Or the next one after that. It doesn't matter. What matters is that the effort is made, and continues to be made, until it becomes easier and more natural.

Successful flirting is about making someone else feel special, good, and wonderful. And it's contagious. Give yourself a chance to do it right. Once you get the hang of it, you'll have a blast.

Chapter 4
LET'S START AT THE BEGINNING

"You know, you don't have to act with me, Steve. You don't have to say
anything and you don't have to do anything. Not a thing.
Oh, maybe just whistle.
You know how to whistle, don't you, Steve?
You just put your lips together and blow."
Lauren Bacall to Humphrey Bogart in *To Have and Have Not*

If it wasn't you, it may have been your kid sister or your best friend or
a next-door neighbor who said, *"Can't I do it over?"* In childhood, you often
can. But, as we get older, our chances for do-overs diminish. The exam you
failed in high school, the job interview that didn't go well, the career that
didn't happen, the one that got away – all gone. As we move into middle-age,
everything is harder, especially starting over. Not only can we not go home
again, the neighborhood is now condos and strip centers! The idea of a new
beginning, doing it again and getting it right feels as probable as climbing
the rocky side of the highest mountain. So let's take a look at the side of the
mountain that's not so rocky!

"Count not what is lost but what is left."
(*Chinese Proverb*)

Ah, romance. Where there's a will there really is a way. Let's talk about
doing it over, but a different way this time. You've paid your dues. And now
that you've entered middle-age, you're not too old to live and love as well as
learn from your past mistakes. Take advantage of the opportunity to reinvent

17

yourself as you move forward. You've come this far, learned so much, given so much, and loved so much. You've earned some stripes.

It doesn't matter whether you're unattached because of divorce, death, bad timing, bad karma, or you haven't yet taken the leap. In a new encounter with someone interesting, there are certain universal rules that we've all learned but frequently forget:

A few flirting essentials, no matter who you are:

1. **A Positive Attitude** – People are drawn to others who show energy, enthusiasm and interest in them. Conversation should be about things that you like, things that they like, and what gives each of you joy. This is not the time to put a wet blanket on potential sparks by referring to things you dislike, past disappointments, or current ailments.

2. **Smile** – Who can resist a smile? Under any circumstances, a smile is a universal invitation, a welcome, and a sign of encouragement. A frown is nothing but a *do not disturb sign* on your face. A smile can be shy, confident or devil may care. No matter, as long as it's there, because what it says about you is that you are approachable, accepting, and nice. Nothing is more attractive than a smile.

3. **Talk** – Silence isn't always golden. Sometimes it's a lead anchor that brings a decisive end to a conversation. Talk is stimulating, especially with lively give and take. Don't hog the stage but offer enough to give some clues as to who you are. Ask open-ended questions that draw a person out in conversation, not yes and no questions that sound more like an inquisition. The more you get him to talk, the smarter he'll think you are. Finding a few good questions to initiate a more meaningful conversation is worth your time if you don't want to fall victim to the typical *20-questions* routine that is stale, expected, and boring.

4. **Listen** – Nothing makes a man think you're interesting more than when you are interested in him. Listen to him. But don't just listen, waiting for your moment to take back the conversation. Listen and care about what he has to say. Ask probing questions to draw him out on topics that seem to interest him. And while you're listening, don't *pull focus* by trying to bring the conversation back to you. If he's interested, he'll eventually get to you on his own, once the flattering topic of his life is sufficiently explored. And if he doesn't come back to you, maybe that's a clue. Is this a man you want to pursue? After all, not every prince will be charming, and you have a right to move on, find someone else to charm and someone who you would like to charm you.

5. **Eye Contact** – When you look at a man and hold his eyes, you are saying, *"you matter to me and have my full attention"*. That should get *his* attention! Scanning the room to see if there are others more interesting is a turn-off, and broadcasts that you're shopping around. It's a bad way to try to interest a man. Stay focused, stay tuned to him, and he will most likely stay tuned to you.

6. **Touch** – A little human contact goes a long way. A handshake that lingers, a touch on the arm, a brush of fingertips is nice, not naughty. But take your cues from him. If he chooses to keep his distance, don't slip into his side of the table and encroach on his space. If he touches your arm to help you to your seat, don't shirk his arm away. Think of yourself as friendly, but not cloying; welcoming without being hungry. Touch, at this point of the encounter, needs to be handled carefully so as not to give offense, or the wrong idea. But gentle touch lets him know you aren't rejecting him, and might welcome something more, eventually.

7. **Body Language** – Uncross your arms (mental and otherwise). In business, when you lean forward, arms on the table in an open position, it means you are willing to discuss, interested in the topic and the person, and generally agreeable. It's the same in romance. When you lean back, cross your arms and pull inward, you convey you are closed to this encounter. To invite someone in, don't resort to defensive gestures that may give the wrong impression. You want to be open (if you are indeed open) to this relationship. Step outside yourself and objectively notice your body language to make sure you are saying what you want to say, in the right way. While words are important, our body language and demeanor often creates greater misunderstandings and confusion than anything we ever say.

8. **Avoid Certain Topics** – Such as how you dote on your cats, why you hate your ex, or your myriad of health problems. Save your opinions on the state of the world, finances, politics, or your children for another time, when he has shown interest in getting to know you better. Why spoil a good evening with negative information that makes him think, *"Geez, I don't need this!"* Better to wait until he's a bit more engaged in who you are, before you reveal points in controversy, warts and all.

We concede that it's not easy, for men or for us. It's not unusual to be self-conscious of your behavior and have difficulty feeling at ease. There are many ways to make a first impression, and sometimes you have no clue what's occurred. You may not realize you're setting a tone and creating a dynamic that's completely unintended. Men are often as insecure as we are, and also struggle to interpret signals. Some of their responses may surprise you, but watch carefully to make sure you are not being misunderstood.

We've heard men comment:

- "I don't think she liked me. She never smiled once."
- "I tried to engage her in conversation, but she was always looking around the room as if she hoped she would see someone better."
- "I thought we were getting along great, but then I saw her glancing at her watch as if she couldn't wait for the evening to be over."
- "Every time I tried to open the door, pull out her chair, or help her with her coat, she seemed to tense up."
- "She was nice, I suppose, but I don't think she said ten words all night."
- "It wasn't exactly that she was smug. It was this look, like I should feel lucky she was willing to give me a few hours of her precious time."
- "It was very uncomfortable. I knew her a minute and a half and suddenly she was holding onto me and not letting go."

Dating is awkward. We may be rusty and being ill at ease can come across as rude. Even worse is that we often make ourselves crazy by second-guessing. In our younger dating years we may have obsessed over how our hair looked, the size of our breasts, whether we came across as too prudish or not prudish enough. A lot of us fretted over whether we were too smart, too clever or two quick, remembering our mother's admonitions to *not be too smart*.

Now we worry about crow's feet, weight gain, age spots, being too affluent (or not affluent enough), being grandmothers and thus considered a turn-off, coming on too strong too soon, being divorced once, twice, or thrice too much or whether his kids (or yours) would even approve, just to name a few. Add that to the myriad of other insecurities about getting older, and it's no wonder we aren't at ease putting our best feet forward. Our feet are now sporting comfortable shoes! But so are theirs.

No doubt you're seasoned, experienced, and have been around the block a few times. But this is unchartered territory and there's a lot to learn. Every person and situation is different. Are you getting a lot of yawns, uh huhs, and clock watching? Is the time dragging and you need an exit strategy? Or are more questions being asked to make the evening linger? Watch the cues, or as the poker players say, watch for the *tell*. If it's working, great. If it isn't, at this age you can cut your losses and the evening short. If you're confused about the signs, ask for clarification. Signs are signs and you need to learn how to read them. If he's *"just not into you"*, don't ignore it. At this stage, it makes no sense to make excuses or pretend you don't know.

What would you do?

You meet what you think is a great guy at a Sunday night dinner party. You know he's divorced, lives alone and is available. He's pleasant and entertaining but you know nothing about his emotional or financial stability. The topics of discussion have varied but neither of you has touched on anything personal nor brought up the idea of seeing one another again.

After an engaging conversation at the table, the party adjourns to the living room where the two of you have commandeered the love seat. You notice he looks at his watch and mentions he has a busy week. You also need to leave but he hasn't yet asked for your number. Hmm? Would you dial up the flirtation or cut your losses and get your coat?

If you've engaged in a conversation for a while, and like what you've seen and heard and he hasn't bolted for the door, what might you do?

Let's try some of these scenarios on for size:

1. **You tell him it's been lovely meeting him, thank your hostess, say good night and walk toward the door hoping he'll leap up to remind you he needs your phone number.** This is a cautious approach, certain to not embarrass you, but it's up to him to take the next step and up in the air as to whether this will end productively.

2. **You smile, tell him how much fun you had talking with him, lightly touch his hand in a seemingly casual way, and mention that you hope you will see him again, sometime.** This is confident and cautious and still appropriately flirtatious, letting him know you'll take his call. It's an invitation without being too exposed. It lets him know he won't be rejected if he makes an effort to pursue you.

3. **You ask him, if he's not too tired, would he like to extend the evening just a wee bit more and go someplace for a drink?** This is definitely a confident and daring approach. It's bold and completely acceptable, but you have to be prepared for him to decline. If he does so, no harm done, your ego is still intact and the ball is in his court.

4. **You tell him you have to leave but would love to continue what has been a stimulating conversation and offer to exchange numbers to get together another time.** This is a relatively low-key flirtation, but with the guts to take a chance. If he gives you his number, take it. If he asks for yours, give it. Tell him you'll look forward to hearing from him.

Let him take the initiative to call. And if he doesn't, keep it for future reference if you ever host a dinner party and want to include him.

5. **You suggest you exchange email addresses and keep in touch.** This is another form of cautious with a hint of interest, but also a bit more distance. The email approach is cooler than the phone, and less involving. If you do hear from him or him from you, see if he is willing to go to the next level. You don't need a pen pal.

6. **You shift your position to sit closer to him, lower your voice and tell him what serendipity it's been to meet someone so nice in such an unexpected way.** This is very flirtatious bordering on coquettish, and if it works, you go girl! Certainly, he will get the drift that you are interested, but it may also give the impression that you are willing to go further than flirtation. Handle this carefully so you don't give the appearance of offering more than you bargained for. On the other hand, maybe you are, but just be prepared to take responsibility for it. Honestly.

7. **You ask him if he's interested in seeing you again.** This is direct sink or swim. It's clear, unambiguous, and if he's honest, you'll get your answer then and there. We presume if you ask such a question, you have an inkling of the answer, and that he will say yes.

8. **You thank him for helping to make it such a lovely evening, give him a friendly hug and say your goodbyes.** This is sincere and sisterly and possibly doomed if you come across as working the room like at a charity function or business meeting. In order for there to be a flirtation involved, you have to give him a little something extra that you don't give to just anybody or everybody at the party, something to make him feel special.

9. **You tell him you think he's hot, and then wait for his reaction.** This is as bold as it gets, and declares your interest, no doubt about it. He will certainly be flattered, appreciate the compliment and may just jump at the chance to prove it!

10. **You look bored, stare around the room looking for someone more interesting to talk to or reach for your purse.** This is Adieu. The kiss of death. Only a masochist will try to climb your icy mountain.

The moment should dictate the attitude; the attitude shouldn't dictate the moment.

The occasion and mood should dictate your conduct. So often people make the mistake of acting the same way under different circumstances. The soft, teasing giggle is perfect when the evening conversation has been light. But if the subject turns serious, so must your style. You don't have to get maudlin or academic or angry, but your tone should fit the topic. It seems so obvious, but if it were, why do we see so many painfully embarrassing moments where the moment is *off kilter?*

Remember when we were in middle school and self-conscious about boys? Remember the girls that would laugh all too loudly, be exaggerated in their gestures and draw attention to themselves in the halls? This behavior was always intended to get the boys to notice. We don't have to do that anymore. They notice. They really notice, even when they pretend they don't.

It's not hard to get men to notice you.

In fact, they already do. It's likely you just don't notice them noticing you. Men try to be discreet because like all of us, they fear rejection. They see you enter the room but avert their eyes because they don't want to appear crude. While you think they are unaware of your charms, and come off as overly insensitive and boorish because they don't understand your cues, you can help set the stage and create an opening for men to feel more at ease if you try some of these suggestions.

Try these on someone and soon you'll discover if he's game or ready to pass:

1. **Get close enough to let him get a whiff of your perfume or soap.** Don't be cloying in your scent, as it may be a turnoff. But the fresh, clean scent of a woman is hard-wired into a man's DNA and can be both powerful encouragement and a powerful aphrodisiac.

2. **Smile (or even laugh), at his attempts at being funny.** You don't have to guffaw, but when he makes an effort to amuse, you can show your appreciation by a friendly response. If you groan, act horrified, or cut him off, he will not make the effort again.

3. **Gently touch his face, hand, hair, or arm.** The sense of touch is disarming. It doesn't have to be a death grip, but letting him know you aren't averse to physical touch is compelling for him.

4. **Ask questions, and show him you're listening, actively.** Nothing makes him think you are wonderful more than when you make him feel wonderful, by paying attention to what he has to say. Conversely,

nothing makes a man feel more insignificant than when you are tuned out, just waiting to jump in with your own monologue.

5. **Pay him a sincere compliment that is unique to him.** If he does or says something that pleases you, be specific and say so. "I like that you told them you hated the plan when someone else wouldn't have had the nerve" is just the kind of thing that will get you more of what you like and let him know you like him.

6. **Close the space between the two of you and adjust closer, or not, depending on his reaction.** If you have any interest in him, and sense that he may be interested as well, why not scoot a little closer, letting him know you aren't afraid or offended by closeness, to him. If he moves away, take your cue and do so as well.

7. **Be self-assured but not self-absorbed.** Of course you want some of the conversation to come from your side of the table, but you don't have to hog it either. You are entitled to have opinions, and when you share them, do so in the spirit of conversation, not heated debate. The point is to find common ground, show you respect each other's points of view, and continue the discussion to include other topics of interest. The fine art of conversation allows for different viewpoints, and welcomes a good discussion.

8. **Watch his reaction to the idea of doing something together in the future.** Maybe it's too soon to talk about taking trips together, but catching a movie, going to a game, taking a walk to go leaf peeping are all lovely things to think about, that are non-threatening. Asking to meet his children may be a bit forward at this time, but it wouldn't hurt, if it came up, to respond with, "that would be nice, sometime."

9. **Let him know you had a good time.** If you enjoyed your time with him, let him know, and why. "You are such a great conversationalist, you are such fun to dance with, and the evening just seemed to fly by" are all good ways to let him know you had fun, and that you'd welcome another encounter.

What about you? Has he shown the appropriate interest? Be on the lookout for things you should expect from his reaction:

1. **Does he show an interest in your story too, or is it all about him?** While you are being attentive and listening well, is he at all interested in you? Does he ask questions and draw you into the conversation or is it all about him? If he is clueless that he is being self-absorbed, you can be

pleasant and gracious and cut the time short. *"Gee, would you look at the time?"* is not a bad thing to say if it's not going anywhere but down.

2. **Does he make you feel inferior to him in any way?** Sometimes men can be impolite or rude or downright cruel. Sometimes it's subtler. Pompous. Arrogant. Self-important. Don't waste a moment trying to figure out why, analyze him or forgive him. Move on. Why permit any man to make you feel bad? Since he can't do it without your participation, run, don't walk, from this encounter.

3. **Does he have a sense of humor?** When women are asked what the most important attribute in a man is, humor comes up as one of the top three. Without a sense of humor, how can a person get through the challenges of life, especially at our age? We need humor to survive, and cope, and put life into perspective, particularly when it isn't fun. Being with a person that is joyless is a dull proposition. Move on!

4. **He doesn't have to be Brooks Brothers, but does he make an effort at being clean and presentable?** Sometimes men need a little *woman's touch* to help them with a sense of style. Is he educable? Does he seem unaware of his appearance or defiant about it? Is he making a conscious statement to be unkempt or does he not realize he is too casual? If it looks like he will be a project, think twice before taking it on. If you have to become his mother, coaching or scolding him to bathe, brush his teeth, or more, think about if you need or want that at this time in your life.

5. **Does he notice you and comment favorably on what he sees?** Does he appreciate how you look, how you think, the nice home you've created, and the dish you prepared? Does he compliment you sincerely and make you feel good? If so, that's a very good sign, but if he is loathe to parse out a compliment, especially when you know you deserve one, then that may tell you he is emotionally withholding, and you should wonder why.

6. **Does he listen to what you say and get involved in drawing you further into the conversation or cut you off to bring the conversation back to him?** Is it all about him or does he care about what you have to say? Does he respond to your comments or carry on his own monologue, interspersed with an occasional pause for breath? Does it always have to be about him or can he leave his own ego at the door long enough to recognize yours? A man who is all about himself will always be about himself, and women are merely accessories to the crime.

7. **Is he affectionate without being presumptuous or forward?** Beware of those *darling, sweetheart* or *honey* types that come on too strong, too soon. It's nice to have someone express terms of endearment, but if offered too soon, they come off as insincere and empty. One has to earn them to enjoy them, and they should be expressed when the relationship moves to the point when they are natural, not robotic.

8. **Does he demonstrate that he's stable, smart, and self-sufficient?** If he seems grounded, thinks things through, and is not needy, he may well be someone to get to know better. But don't ignore signs of instability. Be sure to give your guy an objective once over.

9. **Does he make it clear that his interest goes beyond the moment?** If there is any spark to the connection between you two, and he indicates he is interested in seeing if it can burn brighter, then you have a clear and uncomplicated sign that he's interested, and it's up to you to help take it to the next level or date.

10. **Does he take the initiative in suggesting another time to be together?** See if he is making plans to get together again or using his busy schedule as an excuse. Is he pulling out his Blackberry or calendar to pick new dates or making excuses about calendaring problems? Remember, getting together doesn't have to be about dinner, it can be lunch, breakfast, drinks or a walk. If he's only willing to pencil rather than ink you into his calendar, move on. We're all busy, and when we care about someone we figure out how to make time in our lives.

**"The beginning is the most important part of the work".
(Plato, *author, philosopher*)**

Your days of being pursued for your amazing legs, firm breasts or pretty face have been replaced. You are now desired for other fine qualities: a sense of humor, good character, intelligence, experience, kindness and joy. Ignore the age spots, cellulite, hard to lose pounds, hair loss, wrinkles, and fatigue. The men we want have them too, and still we find them attractive. Younger people can be cute and coy in their search for Mr. Right. But at *50-plus*, it's essential to be your authentic self, because there is nothing more right than a confident woman. And the more you are yourself, the greater the likelihood you'll meet that one special man who's looking for a woman *just like you.*

Chapter 5
IT'S A BIG WORLD AFTER ALL

"Life can never give security, it can only promise opportunity."
Chinese proverb

No doubt you've said or thought some of the following:

- "The good ones are taken."

- "I'll never meet someone."

- "No one wants an over-the-hill person like me."

- "There's no place to go to meet anyone decent."

- "I don't look good enough for anyone to want me."

- "My time for love and romance has come and gone."

- "I'm not going to find happiness by going to a bar."

Blah, blah, blah! We've heard these lines or ones like them, endlessly. If you believe them, stop. Don't make negativity a self-fulfilling prophecy.

Henry Ford once said, *"If you think you can you can. And if you think you can't, you're right."* Nowhere is this truer than in the arena of dating, flirting, and meeting the right person. There are no guarantees that you will be successful in any of them, except the guarantee that if you do nothing, nothing is what you'll get.

If you are willing to participate in this game called love (or at least flirtation) you can meet someone, you will meet someone and even the good ones get recycled. Aren't you a *good one?* It's half attitude and, yes, half being at the right place at the right time, which logically leads to the question, when and where is that?

Is there just one place? No. But the wrong place is hiding out in your house flipping the TV remote. There are so many places where an interesting person can be found that it boggles the mind where to start! You can find these places and go to them with minimal effort. Not everyone is coupled up like Noah's Ark. Interesting, and interested, singles want a life, too, and are out there pursuing an abundance of activities that are also available to you.

What do you enjoy? What would you like to learn? Where do you want to go? If you start with what would hold your attention, most likely you'll feel more at ease, and be more yourself. These are some of the first places to consider as you embark on finding some good flirting material.

So what do you like? What about the gym, acting classes, a lecture on wine collecting, a new exhibit at the museum, a course at your local college, a bridge club, hiking on nearby trails, or volunteering for a political candidate? What about learning a language, sitting on a Board, starting a garden, or taking a writing class? Ever consider a class on digital photography? Want to be a better swimmer? There are people, just like you, who do any and all of these things, and more. There is no limit to the possibilities of where you may meet your stranger, besides across a crowded room!

Consider some successful serendipitous meetings places others have enjoyed:

- Adjacent seats on an airplane *("Would you recommend that book?")*

- In the supermarket *("Did you check out the size of those tomatoes?")*

- Art gallery reception *("There's something calming about this painting, don't you think?")*

- Parking garage of the mall *("I'm lost, again.")*

- Evening classes at the local college *("Did the dog eat your homework too?")*

- Business networking dinner *("I don't know a soul here. Can I say hello to you?")*

- Blind date *("My friend said I'd enjoy meeting you, and she was right.")*

- Matchmaking service *("I'm not just any old desperate housewife, you know.")*

- Blood donor visiting sick patient *("I wanted to give him the shirt off my back but it wouldn't fit.")*

- Vacation encounter *("I'd kill to hear some English!")*

- At a wedding *("So, bride or groom?")*
- At a funeral *("How did you know the deceased?")*
- At a Board meeting *("Do you serve on other Boards as well?")*
- At a dog run *("Cute dog. And the owner isn't too bad either!")*
- A hiking trail *("Got Band-Aids?")*
- At the pool *("Are you the type that dives or inches your way in?")*
- On a cruise *("Is this your first time cruising?")*
- In a veterinarian's waiting room *("That's a beautiful cat.")*
- At a film festival *("What did you think of the movie?")*
- At a bakery *("How are the cupcakes?")*
- In a Starbucks *("What's a Chai Latte?")*
- At a party *("Care to dance?")*

Being in the right place, at the right time, with the right words only entails making the small effort to get out of your rut and loosen your tongue.

**"They keep saying the right person will come along.
I think mine got hit by a truck."
(Anonymous)**

The opportunity for flirtation and romance is everywhere. It's your attitude that will determine the outcome. If you've made the decision that you're not destined to ever meet anyone, you won't. If you are open and receptive to the possibilities, the possibilities are unlimited.

Cynicism masks a lot of insecurities and fears. Worse, it inhibits you from taking advantage of the possibilities that exist if you are receptive to your surroundings and attentive to the people you encounter. You won't get far if you walk through the world with blinders, being too selective about what and whom you let into your world, and discounting people too quickly because they don't fit some profile you've constructed. The best surprises are surprises!

You might be astonished to learn that the unmarried owner of your pest extermination company has a degree in music and loves opera as much as you do! Or that the attractive plumber who appears a bit rough around the edges, is more financially stable than the GQ gent you met at a local watering hole the night before. Looking for Mr. Doctor, Lawyer or Chief Operating Officer keeps the prospect pool a bit too shallow. Many of those who earned professional degrees have opted to open restaurants, small businesses, become tradesmen/craftsmen or investors in their own properties instead of taking on the traditional prestige labels. By keeping an open mind and not leaping to conclusions, you are as likely to meet Mr. Right at a neighborhood recycle center as at your friend's Christmas party.

Many of the most meaningful meeting moments occur when you least expect them, and often when you don't look your best because you aren't trolling but rather going about your daily business. Some of the most serendipitous encounters occur when you don't have any makeup on, are sweating from a workout, or your hair is pulled back in a scrunchy. Your guard is down, you have no expectations, and sometimes the magic happens when you're just living your life.

Janet's Story

Janet, a successful businesswoman who just rounded the corner on sixty, was hit hard when her husband of 30 years announced he was leaving. And this was but one in a series of alarming discoveries. A look in the mirror made her acutely aware of each one of her 60 years. This otherwise confident and sophisticated woman found her self-esteem had vanished overnight and she was awash in self-pity.

Efforts to coax Janet out of this malaise were greeted with: "I don't know how to do this (dating) anymore, if I ever did. I've been married my entire adult life. I don't know how to talk to a man. I don't know how to flirt. I feel so beaten down that even if I try, I know I'll fail and make a complete fool of myself."

After several long lonely months of sorrow, Janet knew she needed to pull herself together. She agreed to join a local gym with one of her friends. Fearing she looked too lumpy in a leotard, she purchased baggy sweats. Two nights a week she dragged herself to the health club where she knew no one and embraced her anonymity while she burned off the calories.

One evening, an attractive 60-something man approached her and asked if she'd like to have coffee after her workout. She was stunned and flattered and without a pause, said yes. After they agreed to a later time and place she realized she hadn't really even noticed what he looked like, and wasn't sure if she'd recognize him again!

When she arrived at the coffee shop at 9 PM, she didn't know him, but he knew her. He was fit, recently divorced and clearly had been checking her out. Coffee together was pleasant; she enjoyed the attention, and felt relaxed in his company. If he'd been interested in her sans makeup and fashion, he seemed to like the cleaned up version as well. Was it magic? Not really. But the one-hour flirtation helped her begin to regain some sense of self again.

He didn't call later, but it didn't matter. His brief interest helped Janet dip a toe into the pool and that made it easier for her to envision wading up to her waist in the future.

Janet could have beat a hasty retreat after her first venture into the singles world ended before it began. But she told us it gave her just the boost of confidence she badly needed. If a man could want to meet her when she was in sweaty, baggy clothes, with her hair a mess and no make-up, it meant she still had it and was not yet done with the world of romance. She and her gym stud had little in common, but that didn't mean the next man wouldn't share her interests. This smart businesswoman used her head to open up her heart for new possibilities.

"We all stumble, every one of us.
That's why it's a comfort to go hand in hand."
(Emily Kimbrough, author, lecturer and former radio commentator)

Vicky's Story

Vicky was fat, pure and simple. She went to Weight Watchers and Jenny Craig and every other diet group she could find. Her husband hadn't come near her in years. She pretended all was okay and denied the voice that told her it wasn't. When finally served with divorce papers she told her friends that it was her own fault. After all, look at what she had allowed herself to become at the age of 58.

For a year after her divorce she threw herself into the many charitable activities that had always given her pleasure and purpose. She volunteered her time at hospitals, reading to children and the elderly. She worked at hospices and spent the summer volunteering at a camp for handicapped children. She gave her love where it was needed and where she was appreciated, regardless of her size.

One day at the hospital, Anthony, a 65 year old widowed pharmacist approached her to say, "I've watched you for three months and I've never seen a kinder person. You must be a saint. Would you have dinner with me one night?"

Anthony was sweet, gentle and kind, though he talked with a slight lisp and resembled a skinny Dom DeLouise. Vicky found him amusing and endearing. She's still fat. He's still skinny and lisps. Anthony said he met a saint. Vicky said she found the sweetest man in the world. And they're still happily together, after three years.

A good attitude, getting out there, and a little confidence can take you miles away from where you start. We know it's difficult. We know you can't just flip a switch and voila, you're transformed into this confident, assertive woman ready to face the dating world.

It's OK to be scared. No one said it's easy. We simply say it's possible.

Chapter 6
BACK IN THE SADDLE, AGAIN

"I seem to remember you from one of my dreams. One of my better ones."
Dick Powell to Anne Shirley in *Farewell My Lovely*

Anna's Story

At 55, Anna was finally finished with a divorce that took over a year to conclude. To flesh out her alimony and child support for her two high school daughters, she worked part time. As long as she adhered to a modest budget, she could manage. Once she started to get her life into a comfortable routine, she was optimistic she'd meet someone with whom to share good times.

While out walking her dog, Anna spotted a new neighbor moving in three houses down from hers and she wandered over to welcome him to the community. Steven, 63 and a widower of five years, didn't look half bad. She didn't want to seem forward, but here he was, practically next door, with a shy smile that made her smile back. So she took a shot and invited him to come over for coffee and cheesecake, when he was ready to take a break from unpacking. Charmed by her offer, he was over in an hour.

When he arrived, coffee was ready, and Anna looked nice. She used the hour wisely!

"He's cute," she thought.

"She's nice," his smile said back to her.

Conversation flowed easily between them and as if on cue, Steven invited her for dinner the following Saturday night. For the next few days, Anna wavered between excitement and anxiety. What to wear, what to say, what to do? When she drove past his house, she slowed up, hoping to have an opportunity to spontaneously say hello. When she didn't see his car, she wondered what he was doing, or with whom.

Saturday night arrived and Steven showed up promptly, looking great. If Anna had scripted the evening, it couldn't have gone better. He was urbane and charming; a perfect William Powell to her Myrna Loy. When he took her home, there was a kiss at the front door that made her feel twenty again. "I'll call you," he said. "I'd like that," she answered. For the first time in a long time, she felt something stir. With relief she thought: I've been dormant, not dead!

But then the waiting began.

Would he call tomorrow? Should she call and thank him, bake him cookies and leave them on his doorstep? Leave a poem in his mailbox? What should she wear on the next date? What if he wants more than a kiss? What if he doesn't?

By day three, with no word at all from Steven, the questions intensified.

Did he really enjoy himself? Would there be another date? Did she misread his interest? If he didn't like her, why did he kiss her that way? Is he away on business and that's why he hasn't called? Is he involved with someone else and lied when he said he wasn't? Has he fallen down, broken bones, and sprawled on his kitchen floor praying she'll come by to save him? If he had to go out of town, wouldn't it have been polite to tell her he'd be gone for a week? Was it all a lie? Is he a sociopath? A Casanova?

Her confidence faded to reveal her underlying insecurities and self-doubt.

After a week, she was ready to put him into the category of liar, game player and creep. Anna slowly drove herself (and every friend she had) crazy with her second-guessing, detail-analyzing, obsessive behavior-asking, "What did it mean, why did he do it, how can you ever tell what is and isn't real?" If she weren't history already, she would have been if Steven could read her thoughts.

Three weeks passed and Steven surprised Anna with his call. Resisting the urge to respond with a frosty and accusatory retort, Anna instead offered a warm greeting and the conversation eventually turned to his interest in a second date.

As it turned out, the second date was better than the first but Anna wondered if again she would have to wait three weeks to see him.

At Anna's front door, the kissing lasted longer and was better than last time. Anna hasn't had the nerve to ask Steven about why he didn't call sooner but it was still there, a little annoying tickle, at the tip of her consciousness. Her conflict about inviting him in was resolved by the fact that her girls were home. But it bothered her that while she wanted him to stay, she was unsure if the interest was truly reciprocal.

Then she thought fast, and smart. "My kids are away on a ski trip next weekend. Would you like to come over for dinner and we could rent a movie?"

Steven grinned and said, "That sounds great. I'll bring the wine." For the next three months, they got together once or twice a week as it reached a rhythm that almost resembled a couple. Their growing intimacy was lovely, but still, Anna felt there was something missing. She wondered, what does he do with the other 5-6 nights a week when we aren't together?

> **"Never assume that the guy understands that**
> **you and he have a relationship."**
> **(Dave Barry, *humor columnist*)**

About starting over – kisses happen. And sometimes that's all it is, kisses. Sometimes a date is diversion. Sometimes it's a chance to test the potential for the future. Is it good enough to try a second date? A first date can be kismet. Often it's not.

Sometimes he doesn't call because he knows that, as women, we put a lot of meaning in frequency. And maybe the message he wants to impart is *"this is nice, see ya."* Or maybe he will call out of the blue.

And when he does call, how should you play it?

- You can thank him for the last time and mention what a lovely time you had.

- You can say you'd love to get together again and make him feel welcome back in your life.

- Or you can give him the cold shoulder, be sarcastic, scolding and rude; guaranteed to give you a moment's satisfaction, and a solo seat watching Lifetime TV on Saturday night.

Treating a man poorly because he doesn't call on your timetable not only will get you nowhere, it will ensure that you will never hear from him again. Men don't want to run the gauntlet of bad attitude. There are plenty of other women who won't dish it out and most men will seek the path of least resistance.

So, has Anna been taking good advice or following a more negative path? Although Anna glowed most of the time, when she didn't hear from Steven, she moved into glowering. This time, when the phone didn't ring for an entire week, Anna left Steven one message after another. After three unreturned messages, she suspected the tide had turned, he was cooling down and she decided to put her feelings on ice as well.

Two weeks later, Steven called to explain he had been busy with work, his elderly mother and arranging for construction on his house. After dating for three months, and not calling for five weeks, she got the message. She's the woman Steven sees when it's convenient.

Should she drop him? That depends. If Anna enjoys his company, on whatever level, why not continue to do so, albeit on less demanding terms? Until she has someone else to date, Anna can continue to enjoy a companion as something less than a committed relationship. If she feels used, she can terminate it. If she doesn't, then what's the harm?

New insights for dating:

1. What's the rush?

In our 20s, 30s and 40s, there were a number of time-sensitive considerations that aren't applicable anymore. In our early years, we wanted to start families, build careers, put down roots and accumulate stuff. Now, our biological clocks are no longer the issue! The pace can slow down and we can take our time. But time is running out, you say? You haven't got time to waste? That's true, but rushing the process only guarantees that you will make ill-advised and hasty choices, and there is less time to recover from those mistakes. So slow down!

2. Everyone has history, obligations, responsibilities and baggage from those first 50-plus years.

They don't disappear just because you've come along. Our lives aren't so simple that romance can ignite in an instant. We have to fit it into our schedules. Allow for the possibility (probably the fact) that there are other people who are important and things that your new person routinely does that make up his existence. His special people and routines don't stop because you've come along. The same is true for you.

3. Discard preconceived notions about courtship and be open to something different.

Dating is not the priority end-all and be-all of our days. Most of us lead full, if not complicated, lives. No matter when you grew up, there was a formula for dating protocol. But that formula is from a bygone era. It involved people who weren't concerned about pension funds, children, grandchildren, mortgage interest rates, balding, the real estate market, gum disease, the prime rate, graying, cellulite, or a family history of heart disease. Get the picture? Now it's grown-ups dating grown-ups and days get away from us as we struggle to meet our obligations. The second phone call may come a few weeks later, or not at all.

4. Get on with your life and watch how things play out.

If he takes too long to call, maybe it's *adios baby*. But maybe, at a later date, it's flowers, a phone call and an apology: *"My great aunt Esther passed away and I've just gotten back from Nebraska."* Chill out girl, you're not a teenager anymore. If you act like you've been sitting by the phone waiting for it to ring, you will build up resentment toward him, and possibly all men, and disappoint yourself (and him) for being so needy. You're a mature woman, not a clueless youngster.

5. **If you really want to know the answer, *ask!*** To put your mind at ease, why not just be straightforward and ask what you want to know? Yes, go ahead and ask the question if it's burning a hole in your brain. But consider that it might be more judicious to wait until you know each other better. And consider how you would feel if the shoe was on the other foot. Also consider that it may be premature to know just yet what are his intentions. But if you just have to know, ask him. Will you scare him off? It's possible, but not likely. You've earned the right to get answers. Just be aware, you may regret your impatience.

6. **Consider playing it clever rather than coy and cute. There is more than one way to skin a cat.**

   Perhaps, instead of asking your date about the lag time in calling or how soon he will be calling again, you take a different approach. A suggestion that you would like to reciprocate for his kindness by inviting him to a home cooked meal at your home would not be out of line. This way you can test the waters about any future interest in seeing you. Ask him what night would work for him. See if he takes the bait. It's neither presumptuous nor inappropriate; it's just plain neighborly.

For a woman, three or more dates are meaningful. Three or more months of dating are *potential*. For men, it's still practice, though you can easily spot when practice turns into preference. Men aren't that complicated, and not particularly good at hiding their intentions or desires.

What's wrong with going out with someone to simply have a good time? Whether 15 or 50, often we can't help setting up expectations about dating. He loves me, he loves me not. But at our age, it's healthier to quiet those voices. Not every date leads to love. Not every love leads to a relationship. Not every relationship leads to exclusivity, marriage or *happily ever after*. Does there have to be an agenda? Many a young girl envisions being a *bride*. But now you're a woman and being a bride doesn't have to be the objective of every dating experience. You can date because the person is fun, you enjoy his company, you have things in common, and he makes you happy.

Trust your gut.

The fact that you're casually dating one person doesn't mean that you have to shut all doors on seeing who else is out there in the world. You have every right to graze. If you just like one man, play it smart, not desperate. There's a reason why *slowly but surely* has, for many years, been winning the race. But beware: don't try to put a square peg in a round hole. It will never fit.

Don't impose your timetable on the rest of the world unless you want to keep missing the train! Remember that baggage we briefly touched on before? Everyone has a story and that accounts for how we conduct ourselves in life. You can't expect your timetable, expectations and assumptions to be the same as those you meet. Try to understand that we have to adjust to the people we meet just as we need for them to adjust to us.

"Assumptions are the termites of relationships." (Henry Winkler, *actor*)

What happened to Anna and Steven? After dating on and off for a year, Steven had come to appreciate Anna's cooking and her ability to help him see the humor in life's little annoyances. She liked his generosity and eagerness to please. She thought he lacked insight at times and he wished she were more ambitious. They both enjoyed their sex life and he helped Anna abandon her insecurity about her imperfect thighs while she made him feel comfortable about occasional inabilities to perform. After a couple of years, Steven realized he had something special with Anna and wanted to see her more often, maybe even live together. When he suggested they might want to get more serious, Anna surprised Steven by agreeing to give it some thought. It took a few years but Anna had become a smart, confident woman, not leaping until she looked, and looking carefully.

Chapter 7
FOR EVERY BOTTLE THERE'S A TOP

"A particularly beautiful woman is a source of terror.
As a rule, a beautiful woman is a terrible disappointment."
Carl Gustav Jung, *psychologist*

Our friend, Ron, is 63. He's been on the Web meeting women, and his perspective is both seasoned and refreshing. *"You know, the older I get, the more I'm attracted to older women. The gals don't have to look perfect anymore. It's not a movie star audition. I need someone who gets me."* He's not alone in his opinion, which is good news for those of you who are determined to believe that members of the opposite sex are only interested in younger, perfectly shaped, fabulously coiffed women. Look around, and you'll see it simply isn't true.

Many professional models complain that they spend Saturday nights alone and are frequently passed over for dates because men are too intimidated to ask them out. It's ironic, but often perfectly turned out women have more difficulty finding love than those who have, well, some imperfections. These flaws, or *warts*, make us more sympathetic, interesting and approachable. We all have them, though some of us mask them better than others while some don't even try. Still others handle them with humor and soft lights.

"Sex appeal is fifty percent what you've got and fifty percent what people think you've got." (Sophia Loren, *actress*)

Jennifer's Story

"I'm at that awkward age. I look better with my clothes on and the lights off," Jennifer laughed. Through humor and a realistic sense of self, she dates all the time, and men are eager to pursue her. "Thankfully, men don't seem to care as much as I thought they would," she continued. "Between the cellulite, the wrinkles, the sagging breasts and my hair turning gray, I thought I was down for the count in the dating department, but it's just not been the case at all."

Is this unusual? Not necessarily. Jennifer has a lot going for her. She is independent; not clingy, or grasping for a relationship. Her independence is appealing to the men she meets. She's clever. Her candor and humor make her someone to whom men are drawn. She's approachable. Her willingness to date, (to practice, if you will), makes her less threatened (and threatening) by the process and she puts men at ease. She's willing to try. *"It's an opportunity to meet someone and perhaps make a friend,"* she said, *"learn something new, broaden my horizons. I don't click with every man I meet, to be sure, but I can give anyone the benefit of the doubt, at least for lunch."*

More important, Jennifer is realistic. She knows she can't compete with younger women and she doesn't even try. She doesn't hide her age or her life story. She's open. The men she meets aren't put off by a fragile ego. She knows she's not right for everyone, but then, it only takes one. Right?

Times change and, if we're smart, so should we.

Women often accuse men of being shallow in their quest for the perfect mate. But women are often just as fixated on an ideal that more closely resembles fiction as reality. Many women fantasize about the perfect man, and are disappointed when no one materializes to meet those expectations. On the one hand, they complain that there's no one worth dating, and on the other hand they wish, hope, dream, and wait for Prince Charming to magically appear. Fantasies aside, no one comes packaged just the way we want or imagine him to be. He may love baseball while you like opera. He may ride a Harley and the most you've ever risked is a Schwinn. Perhaps he's on a low carb diet and you like to cook pasta. Or he's got a dog and you're allergic.

Realigning your expectations doesn't mean you have to settle. It does mean that you need to be realistic about who you are, and who they are, and adjust accordingly. You can't continue to try to look 30 without appearing ridiculous.

The men you meet should be equally realistic. Down with comb-overs and Speedos. Ditto mini-skirts and ponytails.

If you've attended a high school reunion, you know the shock of seeing all those *old people*. But under the mantle of age may be some real sweethearts who've improved with the years.

Mr. Right may be right under your nose, but if you're stuck in Fantasyland, it's possible you won't recognize him. A wise woman will see the twinkle, the passion, and the light in his eyes.

There is a crass barroom line about how the *"gals get better looking at closing time."* Well, ladies, so do the guys. As we round the corner into our mature years, an interesting phenomenon happens; what used to be considered old and unattractive now looks pretty darned good! What's more, we see things differently now. A full head of hair that used to be a given isn't the criteria by which we size up a man as a prospective date. That he can hold a good conversation and remember your birthday may mean a great deal more.

Biceps that used to make us swoon now don't seem quite as important as just knowing he's healthy and full of life. His *come hither* look may have turned a head or two in the past, but a twinkle of recognition from him that you could share this life together now goes a lot further. Sensible shoes don't mark us as over the hill. They mark us as having *climbed* that hill. Maybe it's nature's way of balancing things out. We may not see as well, even with bifocals, but our ability to see and appreciate character is now pretty keen.

Many middle-aged men want a woman who knows Ella Fitzgerald. They love silver in a woman's hair. A few pounds? Never mind, as long as she puts her hand in his. Forgot her glasses? No problem, he'll loan her his. There's comfort with a woman of a certain age that reassures a man she won't flee when she discovers his shortcomings. He knows there may be a time when he needs her strength to help get him through the day, and he's willing to be there for her when she needs him.

Breast cancer, prostate cancer and diabetes are just a few of the health issues many of us will deal with. It comes with the territory if you're lucky enough to live that long. Taking an attitude of *"Who needs it?"* and avoiding commitment with people your own age, or older, may relieve you of pulling *duty*, but will also relieve you of the rewards of truly caring about someone and having him care for you. With age usually comes wisdom and perspective about what's important. But if you're not willing to care *for* someone, why should he care *about* you?

"Love is like playing the piano. First you must learn to play by the rules, then you must forget the rules and play from your heart." (Unknown)

In middle-age, it's impossible to deny who you are or have become. You've lived your life and it shows on your face, your finances and your health. The time for pretending is over and the need to express your authentic self is at hand. In the 40s and 50s, there were a lot of movies featuring women who set out to marry a millionaire or *get their man* at all costs. Ladies, maybe it worked on the silver screen, and maybe it still does in isolated instances, but don't count on it. Just wanting a man *at all costs* isn't enough.

Remember the old 50s Al Capp comic strip Lil' Abner? For a brief time in his strip there was a chameleon-like character called a "Shmoo, a unique character in that it could physically mutate into anything you wanted it to be. Whether it was a T-bone steak or an easy chair, the Shmoos' sole raison d'etre was to become the exact and literal *object* of desire, regardless what form it needed to take to do so. Sometimes women behave as Shmoos, and it's not an attractive quality because it can't be sustained, as it's not real.

Experience tells us that people who try to become the right person for someone else never present themselves in a genuine way, and the other person eventually will suspect something is amiss and wonder who is really behind the mask. We've heard rejected women who played this game say, *"Why didn't it work? I was willing to do anything to get him to love me!"*

To connect with someone, both parties have to be sincere and vulnerable in coming to the table. It is within the space of such vulnerability that real relationships are born. People can sail under the radar, going from one relationship to another, one date to another. It happens all the time and accounts for much of the unhappiness about not being able to find the right one. Because, to *find* the right one, you have to *be* the right one and put yourself in the place of most potential. If you want to catch a fish, you have to put your line in the water where the fish are. Some will bite. Some you'll throw back. Some will get away. But hold onto the line and persevere. A good catch may take some effort but it's time well spent.

Chapter 8
OLD DOGS AND NEW TRICKS

"Doubt is not a pleasant condition, but certainty is absurd."
Voltaire, *writer, philosopher*

It's scientifically proven that people who continue to use their brains to learn new information such as complicated logic/word/math and thinking games, new languages or cultivate hobbies, do better at staving off the early signs of dementia or Alzheimer's. The *use it or lose it adage* really applies here!

We know that the prospect of starting over is daunting. Change isn't easy. Yet we learn new things all the time. It's necessary to survive. Sometimes we even like change! We know women who have taken up piano in their 50s, program their TiVo's in their 60s, enjoy yoga and Pilates in their 70s and learn to use computers for email in their 80s. Women reinvent themselves over and over, and in so doing, realize that their capacity for learning is only limited by their attitude, not their aptitude.

Why then, should flirting and dating be any different?

When we avoid male/female encounters because we fear looking foolish, we effectively eliminate the potential to embrace and be embraced by new and interesting people. Practically no one reaches middle-age without having had her heart broken, healed and broken again by friends, family, and life in general. Yes, we're scarred. Damaged goods. We've all had our fair share of grief. At this time in our lives why should we be expected to reinvent ourselves in order to meet someone new? It doesn't seem fair. But reinvention isn't just for the purpose of meeting new people. It's about being newly alive and experiencing new adventures. As we cultivate other interests, we become more interesting.

Yes, the old dog needs to learn some new tricks, but learning new tricks isn't simply about programming oneself to switch *on* flirtatious techniques and coquettish mannerisms. It's about opening our minds to the possibility that we have the ability to stretch our boundaries and adapt to change. Our preconceived notions of *what's so* can become the biggest stumbling block to finding happiness.

It's true that the older we get, the more set we are that things should be done a certain way. Usually, we like things the way we like things: safe, expected, and comfortable. So what happens when we need to shake up the status quo and adapt?

"Don't wear that shirt. Don't move those pillows. Don't leave the toilet seat up. Don't squeeze the toothpaste from the middle. Don't put your glass on the table. Don't kiss me when I have lipstick on. Don't mess up my hair. Don't talk with your mouth full. Don't order for me. Don't wear that tie. Don't drive so slow (or fast). Don't sit on my white sofa. Don't move my cheese. In fact, don't even touch it! Don't, don't, don't!"

Is this you? Full of *don'ts* for the men you meet? Or *shoulds, shouldn'ts, can'ts and won'ts?* Are you stuck in rigid ways that don't allow for another's behavioral idiosyncrasies? Do you say no to anything that's different from *your way?* If you're interested in getting back into the flirting game, it's a good idea to *ditch the don'ts* and *shush the shoulds.*

Think old dogs can't learn new tricks? They can. And you will if you want to do something more than watch reruns of *Old Yeller.*

But where to start, starting over? How do you adapt and go from what is to what could be without turning your world upside down? You like things your way but if that means being permanently alone, maybe it's time to learn some new tricks if alone isn't what you want to be.

Do you create a welcoming attitude or do you immediately communicate to a man that he never will be welcomed into your life unless he passes through the very tight knothole of your habits, preferences, behaviors, values, standards and expectations?

Natalie's Story

Natalie is 61, never been married, financially independent and professionally successful. She's had a facelift, dresses well, and has many civic interests. "I'd love to meet someone," she said and wanted some advice on how to go about meeting the right man. Then she countered every one of our suggestions with an objection.

Join a West Coast Swing dance club? Without missing a beat she answered, "I would never meet anyone I'd like there." Take an adult education class on a topic that interests her? She rejected the idea out of hand with "it sounds like too much work." She sneered at the idea of attending cultural Salons saying they "sounded boring". Just talking to her was exhausting! But most astonishing was how clueless she was about her negativity. "I'd love to meet someone" was nothing more than a phrase. Natalie failed to understand that without the right attitude, the great phrase means nothing.

But you're not Natalie, are you? You want to try new things and reinvent yourself and create a new reality. Stop a moment to take inventory.

Have you rejected a man because:

- He wears overalls to work but you prefer Brooks Brothers?
- He sails and you hate the water?
- He's a gourmet cook and you believe the kitchen is a woman's domain?
- He likes Country Western music and you prefer Opera?
- He's into camping and you prefer roughing it at the Hilton?

Step back and take another look. Does he make you feel like a woman? Does he brighten when you walk into the room? Do you brighten when he walks in? Maybe when he scuba dives it's in Greece; a place you've always wanted to visit. Perhaps you'll enjoy having someone cook for you for a change. Ever consider you could like both Country Western and Opera? Loosen up and let new experiences wash over you.

Nowadays, being set in your ways is obsolete. As in nature, we either adapt or die. The ones who adapt, upgrade software and electronics, modify diets, change looks and sometimes even politics. We downsize, right size and reinvent ourselves because it's the way of the world. Evolve. Don't accept limitations. Continue to re-write the rules.

Let's test your tolerance quotient for adaptability:

- If he loves foreign films, do you object and say you don't go to movies with subtitles, or do you thank him for telling you in advance so you can grab the right eyeglasses?
- If he suggests you go for an afternoon hike, do you say that's when you take a nap, complain that you don't have the right shoes, or say, *"what time, and I'll bring the trail mix"*?
- Should he lean in to kiss you and you've got lipstick on, do you turn your head away, pull back to do an *air kiss* or lean into it and think, *guess I'll worry about the lipstick later?*

- When he asks if you play golf, do you grimace and say that there's nothing more boring, or do you say, *"I'm ready to learn"*?
- If he invites you to listen to jazz, do you complain that you don't like the smoke-filled bars and jazz is not really music, or enthusiastically say that you'd *"love to go and who's playing"*?

You know the score. We don't have to add it up. If you are stuck in the paradigm that says you want it your way, and only your way, Burger King can accommodate you at a table for one.

"The ultimate test of a relationship is to disagree but hold hands."
(Eden Penney, author)

See the point? Flexibility and open mindedness are critical to a new start. We're not suggesting you agree to be Bonnie to his Clyde. If Sushi makes you gag, pass on it. And you don't have to go skydiving to prove you're a good sport. You can agree to disagree. But let yourself be open. The man of your dreams is not who you're going to meet. That's why it's a dream! He comes with some good and some not so good qualities, just like you do. He has his own habits, hobbies, familiar behaviors and baggage, just as you do. Don't focus on the negative, and don't demand perfection. The goal in life is not to keep walking in old footprints unless you want to walk alone.

Chapter 9
A LITTLE LIBERATION FROM LIBERATION

"When women are depressed, they eat or go shopping. Men invade another country. It's a whole different way of thinking."
Elayne Boosler, *comedian and activist*

How does it happen that the more we try to be all we can be, we're reminded that if we're too clever, too smart, too successful, and now, too old, we won't be enough – or perhaps we'll be too much – for a man to love us?

Just as we've finally gotten the nerve to toss the lingerie and put on sweatpants, another disconnect has happened. While women have achieved greater gender equality in the boardroom, men have become even more confused in the bedroom as to how to approach the successful woman. Women, on the other hand, are bewildered by what they perceive as a need to be *smart all day, and dumb all night*, in order to find love.

Does a woman have to give up who she is to get what she wants? Though this question is more of a challenge to younger women on the way up than middle-aged women who've arrived, it is a problem.

Many women have become the men they'd like to marry; yet deep down they still look for Mr. Right to be stronger, taller, more successful and more powerful. Unfortunately, often Mr. Right wants a woman, not a competitor, who will adore him.

We are the trailblazers, the bra burners, the women who fought (and still fight) for equality and respect; first for ourselves, and now for our daughters and granddaughters. We've pushed through a lot of glass ceilings and many of us have emerged as winners.

Try as we might, we can't deny that in the unique and complicated arena called love, women and men are different. He likes the hunt. She likes being pursued. How then, after all those years of trying to run the race, do we come to terms with the idea that in order to win, we have to slow down and be caught? But after decades of confused gender expectations, is it any wonder men have gotten a bit lazy in the love department and lost their competitive edge? They don't want to work that hard or try that much. If we want to encourage a bit of Tarzan to our Jane, we have to help them relearn how to be a chest thumper! A little flirtation could set the stage for a comeback and perhaps level the playing field.

In what may be the ultimate irony, men are still attracted to the kind of women who are comfortable being women; not simple, vapid people who need to be rescued, but women who know when to close their briefcases and open their hearts.

No, we're not going to resurrect old tapes from Mom, but we've learned a few things along the way:

- **Men like the hunt.** It's the nature of the beast. It's ingrained in their DNA and our culture supports and reinforces this. But consider, don't we want men who want and need to pursue us?

- **They need to compete and believe that if a woman's worth having, she's worth fighting for.** Nothing makes an object of desire more desirable than the belief that others desire it (her) also. This is also human nature, which is why, when a woman is *busy*, a man wonders *with whom?*

- **When we take away the chase, they lose interest** because they believe that nothing good comes easy. What the heck, we all feel that way, don't we?

Women's liberation accomplished many things, and with the successes, there also came setbacks. When we ignore a man's primordial need to conquer, we stop being the focus, the conquest. Take away the challenge and he's not going to call. If she calls and invites him for coffee, drinks or dinner, what is he hearing? A friendly invitation, or a desperate call to (her) arms?

Joan's Story

Joan met Guy online. She believed he had potential, in spite of both of them being stale at dating. After a few awkward volleys of conversation, they decided to go out. He invited her for dinner Saturday night, thoughtfully well in advance.

He called Saturday afternoon to confirm, which was also considerate. But then came the startling question, "So, whatta you wanna do?"

Surprised, Joan asked, "Did you make reservations anywhere?" Did he have to be reminded of his responsibility in the dating scene?

"No," he said. "didn't think about it."

"Tell you what," she said, trying to be kind, "maybe you should make some calls."

He got the picture, and the reservation.

Joan got the picture too. Guy was socially out of shape. After years of not dating, it's easy to see how a man can get lazy about the protocol. To him, Saturday night was just another night, and going out was just another way to say, *"hey, how 'bout a burger?"* Why are so many men out of shape? Maybe it's because many of us have allowed them to grow flabby.

What do women do wrong? We accept lame excuses for not making plans. We forgive them when they want to go Dutch. Hey, we even suggest it! We make the reservations when they forget. What we don't do is make spending time with us exciting, a challenge, and a chance for them to rise to the occasion and find an occasion to rise to! The goal isn't to achieve more power only to leave men powerless!

We don't have to be strident or militant to prove we're liberated. And we don't have to emasculate men when they are gallant. If we want to meet men who treat women well, we need to be women who like men to treat us well, and with respect. And that means we have to be deserving of that respect. Being liberated doesn't mean we should abandon all rules of decorum. Maybe that was the case in the 70s but it's not anymore.

We shouldn't be so liberated we let them off the hook from wooing us. We may not need it as much as we did when we were younger, but that's not the point. If we want men to do the heavy lifting, we have to let them lift!

Several men remarked, "You'd be surprised by what women do!" Thus, here are examples of some don'ts:

- **Women make the first call.** While that shows you are interested, it takes away his initiative, putting you in the aggressor seat. Initially he may be flattered, but eventually he'll wonder if you plan to be in charge.

- **Women invite sex right away.** Sure, he may want it, if he can do it, but he may also want to set the time and place, and build and enjoy the anticipation. Middle-aged men don't want to be *objects* any more than women do. They also don't need the pressure to perform.

- **Women show up with casseroles,** offer to cook, clean, and render services with little or no provocation. Of course men like the attention, but they don't want to feel guilty or obligated. There is a certain desperation in a woman's willingness to dote on a new man in her life. Not only may a man find himself confused by generosity he has not yet earned, but it may be a real turn-off.

Women want to be cherished, and men want to be adored.

The more accomplished we become, the higher we raise the bar for what we expect from a man. In the mad race to find love after 50, a lot of men are sitting this one out. For many of them, women are way too much work, far too demanding or, ironically, not demanding enough.

We need to find the right balance. We can be smart without being intimidating and work at looking good without being consumed by the endeavor. A man responds to a woman who looks up to him. Admiration is an aphrodisiac. Pointing out his short comings, inadequacies, and foibles may help you feel like you've leveled the playing field, but it also means you'll be playing solo. You may be worrying about him finding a younger woman who puts him on a pedestal, but your real concern should be about becoming the woman who kicks it out from under him. Any woman who makes a man feel ten feet tall will always trump the woman who cuts him down to size.

If we want to be turned on at night after being in charge all day, there's nothing wrong with switching the power button to *off* mode. Leave the rigors of the boardroom when entering the bedroom where men need to feel they're in charge!

"Men play the game; women know the score." (Roger Woddis, *writer and poet*)

If both sides would just get it, there would be less divorce in the world. And what comes first: how he relates to her or her to him? As the stronger sex, it's up to us to set the tone. Are we going to be understanding or shrews? Sexy or cold? Loving or punishing?

Women need to be tender, compassionate, and patient, regardless if they run companies, teach at universities, make records, or set them. We can be as comfortable in silk lingerie as in sweats because we're realists as well as idealists.

We know how to combine the *pragmatic survivor* with a flair for the romantic. Smart women don't harbor illusions as they age, and for the most part, have shifted their expectations from *what if* to *what is*.

A 70s TV commercial claimed, *"If you want him to be more of a man, try being more of a woman."* No point in clenching your teeth at this. It's true.

What happened to women's liberation and equality of the sexes? For one thing, this equality thing is more complicated than we thought.

What does this say about contemporary dating and flirting? It's not a straight line. Men want the hunt but they don't want to be in the wilderness for long. They send mixed signals that drive women crazy because they're filled with the same insecurities that have plagued men forever. To make it worse, the *50-plus* crowd is steeped in old messages and expectations that confuse and confound us as we try to get with the times, but don't know what times to get with!

> **"Sex is like having dinner: Sometimes you joke about the dishes,**
> **sometimes you take the meal seriously."**
> **(Woody Allen, *actor, director, writer, and filmmaker*)**

Help! What's a woman to do? Or not do! In order to put men back in the driver's seat, we need to take our hands off the wheel, but still keep our eyes on the road.

So what if occasionally you purr when you'd prefer to roar! Sometimes you have to give a little to get a lot. Are we contradicting ourselves after all the talk of self-assurance, confidence, and being true to you? Not at all. Mix it up, ladies. There is no hard formula.

The 2005 movie hit, *Hitch* was touted as "Courtship for Dummies" and those dummies were the guys. This was a movie about a guy with a bit of bravado who teaches moonstruck romantics how to snag the women of their dreams. Where is *Hitch* now that we need him to help us find our way?

We long for men who will be unreasonable and outrageous in pursuit of us. We hunger for seduction and romance laced with consideration and sensitivity. We want men who are kind but tough, thoughtful but who take charge. We can run a company and balance the books, and still have our hearts melted by the smart suitor who does it right.

This is a territory with no map, so you have to trust your instincts. Don't be something you're not, but hold back at times when your guy needs to feel in control.

A few guidelines to consider:

- **Men like women who are independent,** but not aggressive.
- **Men want women to talk,** and be good listeners.
- **Men want a lively sex partner,** but not an easy woman. Slow down on the intimacy. By so doing, you show him you're selective, and cautious. And nothing makes a man want you more than wondering if he can

have you at all. Further, nothing makes him drop you faster than thinking, if you're easy with him, then with how many others?

- **Men like smart women,** but don't want to be patronized or belittled if they don't share the same degree of knowledge or experience as you do.

- **A man wants to call *you* if he's interested.** He's a grown up. He's resourceful. He can find your number. And if he can't, what do you want with him anyway?

- **Don't engage in suggestive conversations too soon.** Familiarity breeds contempt, not intimacy. Those not so subtle innuendos may be an overture to sex, and yes, at this age you certainly understand them. You can't play the innocent ingénue. But steer the conversation into safer waters until you know the time is right. "I get where you're going with this, but give me time to figure you out!" could diffuse the moment and buy you time.

- **Don't shoulder the burden of the date.** Let him make an effort. Let him make the plans. Let him be in control. It's a fine line between offering help and taking over. Let him take the lead and you can surrender accordingly.

- **Don't dismiss a man immediately because the initial encounters aren't perfect.** Dating is strange and we're all clumsy at it. Cut him some slack if he stumbles a bit. Give him a chance to get it right, at least once.

- **Do make him feel special.** Dress up for the date. Prepare yourself for an evening out as though you consider him special. Spending time on yourself lets him know you value time with him.

- **Do let him know you view this as a date.** He gets to be the man of the hour, and make the decisions. He's out to show you a good time so let him! Don't complain about the choice of dinner, or the cost or the activity. You may get to choose if there will be a second date, but don't ruin this one!

- **Do let him know you appreciate how he took the time and effort to show you a good time.** Thank him with sincerity, enthusiasm, and sparkle. If he made an effort, appreciate it. Reward good behavior and you're likely to see more of it.

Just because you know the moves doesn't mean you have to play all the hands. You know when you're being natural and you know when you're too pushy. You know when you're being smart or a smart aleck. You know when you're being sincere or desperate, grateful or needy, sensual rather than just plain oversexed. You know!

Being liberated does not preclude being tolerant, smart, and a good listener. You can be reserved and dignified and you can be interesting, beguiling, and alluring. You can be smart when it comes to the flirting game, and, when the time is right, you can plant a red hot *you turn me on* kiss that brings him to his knees. Because, when the time is right, he *will* respect you in the morning!

"I am woman, hear me roar", or not. Figure out if the moment calls for more of a whisper. Then do what you need to do.

Chapter 10
THE RULE OF THREE

"Just because nobody complains,
doesn't mean all parachutes are perfect."
Benny Hill, *comedian*

We've all heard the phrase, *the third time's the charm.* When we meet someone new, it's natural to activate the signals of *Go or No Go.* Many over-50 flirters are impatient to rush to judgment. At our age, expecting love at first sight is a bit naïve. So maybe some men deserve three chances?

The *Rule of Three* refers to the marketing premise that it takes three exposures for a message to actually make an impression. The first time something catches our attention, we think, hmm, interesting. The second time, we think, hmm, this seems familiar and maybe I should look into it. The third time, we think, hmm, maybe I'll give it a try. Dating should be no different.

When two people meet in a social context, rarely are they completely natural. The struggle to be clever, poised, and confident and not appear needy may make some people tongue-tied. Others may be overly cautious and still others ridiculously talkative. Self-consciousness can appear as shy, aloof, self-absorbed or simply dull. Even worse, the effort to seem comfortable can make a person come across as a snob, braggart, or show-off. To fill the silence, a person may chatter on and on about himself. Other times a person may be afraid to ask the other questions for fear of being perceived as prying. Those who are overly eager to convey what they want, what they like and that they are ready for love, may come across as desperate. It's hard too find the right balance, particularly when you feel good about being honest and feel that *time's a wasting!*

At first glance a man may appear not to be your type for a number of reasons. Don't be so quick to write off a second or third encounter. A second look can be an eye-opener. How often, at the early stage of social contact, have you chosen to cut your losses before investing more time in what you believe is an unproductive encounter? A new man may not make your nervous system react like it's been hit by a bolt of lightning (like when you were 20 years old), but if there's even a flicker of potential for ignition, then spending a little more time together may bring some flame to the embers.

"You never lose by loving. You always lose by holding back."
(Barbara DeAngelis, PhD,
author, motivational speaker, and TV personality)

If you're on the fence, make one goal for the first date: to get to the second date. Why? Because some first dates are a disaster. We know a woman, recently divorced, whose first date with a recent widower was waterworks incorporated. They spent the evening taking turns crying about their losses. Though embarrassed at their emotional outpouring, they grudgingly agreed to try one more date. This time, neither brought up their former mates and instead of tears, there were smiles and even a little laughter as they remembered the soggy start they shared.

Still not sure? Shoot for a third date because by then you will know better how you feel. Whether you find a new friend or a new love, at the very least, you'll have gotten some practice in the process of close encounters with the opposite sex. It's all about practice!

Create opportunities to get together under different circumstances. Mix it up. See what he's like in a casual setting, a more formal setting, with other people or just the two of you. This will give you greater insight into who he is and your compatibility. More time together allows you to see not only what he wants you to see but also a variety of moods and reactions to different situations. You will learn what else there is to talk about once you've sifted through your *20 questions* and whether you share interests, priorities, and values. You will also see if that person is punctual, tidy, a planner, or spontaneous. The more time you spend together, the better you'll understand who he is. Information is knowledge and from there you can make a more informed decision.

We've all heard stories about how two people met and instantly disliked each other, only to discover later that they were mistaken and otherwise perfectly matched.

Sylvia's Story

Sylvia was a year out of her divorce. Ben, widowed for 16 years, had dated quite a bit and had become jaded. Sylvia wanted to date, but was still wounded. They met at a community "Salon" and went out a couple of times. Their time together, while pleasant, didn't move the needle. They agreed to be friends. Since they both attended these events, they ran into each other from time to time and enjoyed an occasional conversation. Several months later, Ben called to invite Sylvia to a party at a friend's home – to go as "friends". When he picked her up, he seemed more than a little delighted at how good she looked. She found herself thinking there was something nicely different about him.

At the party, Sylvia was confused to discover that she felt a twinge of jealousy when she noticed an attractive woman talking to Ben. Ben was surprised when, after searching for Sylvia, he couldn't find her. He worried that she had left.

They almost collided at the punch bowl. Sylvia started to say, "I saw you were busy..." as Ben was saying, "I was worried. I thought you had..."

Their mutual annoyance startled them both. Ben and Sylvia were ready to try the dance again.

Too often, for the most superficial reasons, we reject men who could, under the right circumstances, light our fires. Sometimes the dance is ended before we have a chance to see if we like the partner. The jury is still out, but Sylvia and Ben continue to date and the first bad dates are distant memories.

> **"You can't always get what you want, but if you try sometime, you get what you need."**
> **(Mick Jagger, *Rolling Stones lead singer*)**

Have you ever dismissed someone because of any of the following?

- His car is too old, not stylish enough or too dirty.
- His house is too small, not in the right neighborhood or is poorly decorated.
- He smoked pot in the 60s (or didn't!).
- His children have bad jobs, bad marriages or are still living at home.
- His shoes are ugly; his clothes don't fit or flatter.
- He has a mustache, a toupee, or ear hair.
- He thinks Florida is a fun vacation and you think it's a waiting room for what's to come.
- He only reads non-fiction and you're into novels.
- He eats fast food and you're a food purist.

- He's bald, has a comb-over and you like your men *hairy*.
- He wears Hush Puppies and you're into Jimmy Choo.
- There was a spot on his shirt and you think he's a slob.
- His pants are too short and you're a fashion cop.
- His grammar isn't perfect and you wince when he speaks.
- He likes country western music and you're into Sinatra.
- He has a hearing aid or dentures.
- He lives too far away and is not geographically desirable.
- He has a cat and you're allergic.
- He's too short or you're too tall.

The list could go on for days. Just eavesdrop at any table where women are congregated, and you'll hear even more excuses why many men don't make the short list. A lot of women never look beyond the uncut diamond to see the real gem!

Lois' Story

Lois was fixed up on a blind date with Al. When he arrived, she expectantly opened the door. He wasn't what she'd hoped for, and lamely tried to hide her reaction to his hair; not on his head, but on the back of his hands and neck. It went down into his shirt, and she suspected (and cringed) that it most probably blended with a mat of hair on his back. It turned her off so she cut the evening short by faking a headache. Several months later, she attended a party, and there was Al, with a lovely woman as his date. The hair on his neck was cleanly shaved and he had lost about 20 pounds. His hands didn't look as bad as she remembered. In fact, he looked pretty darned good. When they ran into each other, he was pleasant, asked about her headache, and winked knowingly. She was embarrassed and ashamed, and more than that, she noticed he was kind, attentive to his date, and actually more attractive than she remembered. Her snap judgment and early rejection of him cost her the opportunity to be with a partner with potential.

The advantage inherent in the *Rule of Three* is that, with frequency, you get to see each other in different lights: artificial light, moonlight and some natural light. Different views will be revealing, maybe even exciting. Call it three strikes but just remember, calling someone out after only one strike is not fair to him. And, importantly, not fair to you.

Get beyond the urge to be turned off by superficial minutiae and take the time to see what's behind *Door Number 3*. You may not want a *project* but there isn't any man who couldn't benefit from the care and love of a good woman. It might be worth the time and trouble to help turn him from a frog prince into a prince of a guy.

Chapter 11
WOMEN GROW, MEN REMARRY

"Hearts will never be practical until they are made unbreakable."
The Tin Man in the *Wizard of Oz*

Between the years 1620-1699, 128 petitions for separation and divorce were filed in the New England colonies and it was found that women petitioned in 67% of the cases, men in 27% of the cases and both spouses filed jointly in 5% of the cases. That was then, this is now. And guess what! Times haven't changed all that much.

Would it surprise you to learn that men are more likely to stay in a bad relationship than women? As fearful as many women are of suddenly being thrust into independence, men are even more fearful of change. Would it also shock you to discover that more women file for divorce than men? In a psychologists' survey about who initiated the breakup, no matter when the question was asked or of whom, the wife was identified as the initiator in 63-67% of the couples. The husband was identified as the initiator in 26-34% of the couples and in only 4-9% of the cases was the divorce a mutual decision.

The more we change, the more we remain the same. Perhaps women should be labeled the *decisive*, not the *weaker, sex*.

Women are definitely not the weaker sex, so it's time to disabuse ourselves of that age-old myth. True, most of us aren't going to bench press two hundred pounds or volunteer to move a slab of granite, but we're not talking about brawn. We're talking about stamina, stability, survivability and self-awareness. And let's not forget resiliency, for that is what helps us heal.

Dozens of women who are relationship survivors shared some examples of what they did to get back on their feet after a relationship ended.

1. **Talked to friends** about their feelings as well as sought honest answers about how the relationship that had ended was perceived by others.

2. **Read self-help books** to better understand personality types, their own issues as well as exploring options.

3. **Consulted with psychologists/psychiatrists** to help cope with depression, anxiety, confusion, and to find a new direction.

4. **Started taking classes** at a local university. In some cases it was simply to learn subjects of interest but others sought out new careers or made efforts to enhance their skills for better opportunities. This included learning computer skills and how to use the Internet.

5. **Started a new career.** The diversity of employment is rich with choices (and yes, there is a market for bright, mature, organized women). Women found new careers as authors, real estate salespeople, mortgage lenders, caterers, teachers, nurses, lawyers, businesswomen, and even a housekeeper (yes, and she loves it)! From office manager to corporate manager, event planner to motivational speaker, women are reinventing themselves into the careers they always wanted to have.

6. **Joined groups and organizations.** The variety here ranged from becoming active in a charitable foundation, becoming part of a book group, nature walks and lectures.

7. **Volunteered** to help in their children or grandchildren's schools, local hospitals and churches.

8. **Began a regimen** of diet, exercise and self-improvement to take better care of themselves.

9. **Took vacations** to new places, some with tours, some with family members and some alone.

10. **Moved to a new city**, found a new job, met new friends, and got a fresh start.

11. **Slowly, slowly started to meet someone new.**

After a break-up or lost love, mature women typically engage in activities that provide them with some solace and enable them to better understand what went wrong, how they may have contributed to the problem, and how to make better choices in the future. The goal is to grow out of the pain, and into becoming someone who is better equipped and prepared for a new beginning.

However, while women are busy sorting through the carnage of failed relationships, looking for clues to what went wrong and how to avoid the same mistakes in the future, many men rush into remarriage.

"You can only be young once. But you can always be immature."
(Dave Barry, *humor columnist*)

What did men say they did when a relationship ended?

1. **They pretended that all was normal,** *business as usual.*

2. **They distracted themselves** with activities, food, booze or travel.

3. **They rushed to meet someone new,** immediately, to mask their insecurities.

4. **They clammed up** and refused to talk about it, let alone try to figure out how they contributed to the situation.

5. **They assumed they just needed someone *better*.**

6. **They bought a Porsche** (or its equivalent).

Conspicuous by its absence is any mention that women rush to meet someone new.

Many ladies tend to take it slow and steady. They think about what happened and understand the notion that history will repeat itself if they don't learn from their mistakes. For some, the process is about reading a book or two. For others it's as drastic as the need to move to a new neighborhood or new town and start over again. But no matter what approach is taken, it involves the act of becoming more in touch with themselves in order to avoid repeating past mistakes as well as the art of understanding the abundance of choices and opportunities that are there for the taking.

Common factors for the women who successfully find love and happiness after break-ups include:

- The desire to confront what went wrong with the past relationship.

- The need to better understand what role she played in how the relationship went awry.

- Her ability to figure out why she was drawn to the wrong person and acknowledgment that he was the wrong person.

- Her willingness to change direction and avoid repeating her mistake.

- Her refusal to rush into meeting someone new without making sure he passes some basic tests.

- Her re-validation of herself as lovable and desirable, in spite of her ex.

- Her understanding that there is a need to have certain non-negotiable expectations.

"Sexiness wears thin after a while, and beauty fades, but to be married to a man who makes you laugh everyday, ah, now that's a real treat!"
(Joanne Woodward, *actress*)

Men don't necessarily marry for the same reason as women. They hate coming home to an empty house with no hot meal waiting, laundry to be done, an empty and unmade bed as well as an empty refrigerator, bills to pay and another night of re-runs. A man can soon understand the positive side to having a woman around. But it's more than that; a man wants someone with whom he can share laughter and a meal, commiserate about life's downs, celebrate the ups and talk about the day. A mature man wants a woman who's been there, done that and can be there for him. The days of being out on the town every night have come and gone. A home-cooked meal and a companion for the movies or a game of scrabble can make his life less lonely and a lot more enjoyable. Women often fill the void with activities, but a man who is lonely wants a friend and lover.

Loneliness can cloud one's judgment. There's a fine line between filling someone's need for companionship, and being the right companion. It can seem flattering to have a man pursue you, to enjoy all of your time and attention and make you feel desired, and desirable. But it's important to keep a cool head, even when your heart is heating up. Look carefully to see if he is the one to keep your fires going, and going. It may be nice to be needed, but don't confuse need with love.

"Love is a fire. But whether it is going to warm your heart or burn down your house, you can never tell."
(Joan Crawford, *actress*)

Here are some pointers to make sure you can tell the difference:

1. **None of that deja vu all over again!** If the first one didn't work out, hooking up with his clone isn't the answer. Beware the mistake of trying to get it right this time with the same type as the last. Maybe the first time wasn't your fault, but the second time – shame on you.

2. **Does he make you laugh, stimulate you, make you feel good about yourself?** Do you do that for him? If not, what's the point? You don't need someone to fill the easy chair unless he can fill you with happiness and a feeling of comfort. Unless you are the misery loves company type, why choose to be miserable? You can do that all by yourself!

3. **You want a man who wants what you bring to the table.** You can compromise on what movie you're going to see but your job, your family, where you live and how you live are all part of what make you who you are. You shouldn't have to choose what pieces of your life you can keep, in order to keep him. If he wants you to make choices that make you unhappy, you might what to choose to move on.

4. **People don't change much, especially in our older years.** Of course, nuances can change, and do. The desire to make some adjustments in such things as wardrobe, hairstyle, and entertainment has each of us making accommodations to suit the other. But character traits, long held beliefs, entrenched attitudes about money, sex, family, politics, music and more, are some of the areas where there is resistance and no likelihood of change. Either accept him as he is, or plan to be irritated forever.

5. **How charming will those idiosyncrasies be down the road?** Don't look for perfection but if something annoys you to the point of distraction, think about how you're going to feel about that irritating habit in ten years, when it's been repeated a gazillion times. If it bothers you now, it will bother you later, and the fact that you're bothered will bother him. Not an ideal formula for bliss.

6. **Will you resent supporting him, if need be, or will he resent supporting you?** How does the money work? Figure it out before, not after, you get so entrenched in each other's lives. It's important to put all your expectations, values, and attitudes about money on the table so you don't have disappointing surprises. Will he want to leave everything to his kids or will you be taken care of? Does he want you to contribute to the finances? Will you receive an *allowance* or does he expect one? Is it *share and share alike?* Will there need to be a pre-nuptial agreement? These, and many other such questions, must be addressed so they don't become issues when you least expect them.

7. **How is the blend of friends and family?** Not everyone will mesh perfectly but it can't be *oil and water* either. Some of his friends you'll like and some you won't. And some won't like you. How will you handle that? The same goes for your friends and family. Is your

relationship strong enough to work through it? Can you each make an effort when necessary to have a pleasant time with people you might not otherwise choose as friends? It will happen. It's necessary to come together to work through these moments because, otherwise resentment will grow and fester. Don't make him give up others for you, or vice versa. Draw him into your world and make every effort to fit into his. After all, if you can't be on this journey together, you may as well take the trip with someone else.

8. **Does he get who you are? The *real* you?** Life happens. The ups and the downs. Has he seen the bumps, lumps and lines? Has he seen you strained and drained? Have you seen him at his worst? In the trenches, do you crawl away or toward one another? When you are happy does he share your delight or try to bring you down? The passage through the last third of our lives is not a straight line and you want someone who will be there to help negotiate the curves and sharp edges, as well as the easy chair.

"Being deeply loved by someone gives you strength, while loving someone deeply gives you courage." (Lao Tzu, *Chinese taoist philosopher, author*)

Dana and Joe's Story

Dana and Joe met a couple of years ago, and decided to move in together after several months of dating. They have traveled together to many countries, weathered lost luggage and hotels that didn't measure up. They've caught colds and stomach flu, dealt with bad knees and hips and took turns nursing one another back to health. They've argued over money, his kids and hers, how she cooks (or doesn't) and which movies to watch. He's an only child and she's a middle daughter. He reads historical novels voraciously and she reads trashy romance. He sleeps through Opera and she snores through baseball.

And through it all, they laugh.

Their lovemaking is fun and frequent. Their differences are a constant source of amusement rather than division. They are in this together. Neither have any illusions. Over time, more things will likely go bump in the night and each will need help. His virility won't last forever and he'll need her understanding. Eventually, they won't be able to travel as much or make love as long. They are conscious of all this and prepared to cope with life, as it happens. For them, love is not blind. Its eyes are wide open and likes the partner it sees.

Yes, women grow, and men remarry women like you. They marry women who have grown enough to appreciate their own value, and the value they offer to the men in their lives. A good man isn't hard to find – it just takes a good woman to discover where he's hiding.

Chapter 12
IT'S HARD TO FLIRT ON AN EMPTY STOMACH

Let's talk money.

"Money does not make you happy but it quiets the nerves."
Sean O'Casey, *Irish playwright*

If you've passed the *big 50* and you haven't thought about your finances and financial future, the concept of flirting falls into one of two categories: difficult or necessary. This is not where you want to be, or at least, remain.

Though this may sound like one of those late night television infomercials designed to either intimidate or scold you into doing the right thing, the reality is that to a lot of women, money management has been a hit or miss thing. In spite of all our purported liberation, here we are, middle-aged and likely to outlive our money unless we take planning seriously, and seriously plan.

Whether you *ain't got a dime* or have *all the tea in China*, don't think you're exempt from thinking about and planning your financial future. There are a lot of women who still think that their future financial journey involves catching a meal ticket. It's not a plan you should count on, especially if you're *over 50* and just now coming to the realization that money doesn't grow on trees.

Figure out (with assistance if needed) projections for your income over the next 10 to 20 years. Don't start with that lame *"who knows?"* There are people who do and they'll help you. Learn about deductions, capital gains, and interest rates and talk to a trustworthy advisor. They're called financial planners, CPAs, tax advisors, and estate planners.

A good financial planner can help you sort out what you have, what you'll need, what to save and what steps to take. You want to get your financial house in order because bag ladies don't have much of a social life! Let's face it; it's hard to flirt on an empty stomach.

All of us need to do the following:

- **Prepare a budget of your expenses so you'll know how much you spend**. You don't know? This is the first of many reality checkpoints. Unless you have so much money you never need to think about it, a budget keeps you grounded. The purpose is not to put you on an austerity diet but rather to provide you with a perspective on how much you need to cover the lifestyle you have, want or need to accept. By knowing where the money goes, you can prioritize necessary versus indulgence, or *needs versus wants.*

- **Figure out your net income from all sources.** What is left after all expenses and obligations are paid? Be sure your calculation includes the *tax impact* of each source. A good CPA can help you with that.

- **Which is higher, your expenses or your income?** If it's expenses, you're a big girl now, and it's time to make some adjustments. Sooner or later you'll have to pay the piper, so start getting your ship righted now.

- **Do you own or rent?** Live alone or share? Is your home a place that makes financial sense for your future? Would it be better to cash out and take your equity to provide a cushion or keep your house and *let it ride?* Don't get caught up with *"I don't want to move!"* Or worse, "It's too complicated for me to understand!" Sooner or later you will be forced to understand. Reality has a way of doing that, you know.

- **Does where and how you live make health sense?** Is the distance to hospitals, friends, family, or work a potential problem? Are stairs going to be an issue? Is this a good place to be as you move through the *second half?* You may want to be an ostrich and bury your head in the sand, but don't. Pull your head out, consider all your options and keep an open mind. The time to choose well is when you have choices to make. If you choose not to choose, the choice will be made for you and you may not like it.

- **Do you have savings for emergencies?** How much? How accessible are those funds? Have you planned for the unexpected? Don't work from a script that says, *"Nothing's going to happen to me."* No one *expects* accidents. That's why they're called accidents and they happen to each of us, sooner or later.

- **Do you have medical insurance?** Do you know what it covers? Have you applied for all types of medical benefits to which you are entitled such as Medicare? Have you educated yourself about your various choices? Never assume that you know it all. The fact that you've led a healthy life is great but not a *guarantee* that you will always remain that way (though the odds are in your favor if you've taken good care of yourself). The truth is, health insurance is confusing. Knowing what protection you have can be daunting. Don't wait until you need it to see what your insurance covers. We know reading the fine print can put anyone to sleep, but better to take a short nap than experience sleepless nights realizing you have no coverage and didn't take the time to discover that in advance.

- **Prepare a will and/or estate plan.** We know, we know, you're healthy and still statistically young. But estate planning is the responsible thing to do, so do it anyway. A good plan protects you and your heirs, makes for smart tax planning and will lighten the burden on those you leave behind.

"Money, if it does not bring you happiness, will at least help you be miserable in comfort." (Helen Gurley Brown, *author, publisher, former editor-in-chief for Cosmopolitan Magazine*)

Finances and flirting are tied together.

It's a given, that self-assurance and a good self-image will not only make you better at flirting, but more successful at meeting men and taking flirtation to the next level. But there are still other factors to consider. Flirting should convey an attitude of confidence, not desperation.

One element of self-assurance is knowing that your life is in order. As much as some of us hate to admit it, money is a critical part of our lives and that aspect needs to be handled intelligently. Just as money problems frequently are the source of marital problems, the same can be true in the dating world.

You don't have to be rich, thin or gorgeous to meet a wonderful man.

But, you need to take care of yourself, be well-groomed and make an effort. This includes your financial appearance too, and this is one façade that can't be maintained if there's no substance behind it. When the bucks stop, so does the pretense. Better to live responsibly within your means than have your house of (credit) cards collapse.

How can you feel sexy, flirtatious and appealing if you're worrying about any of the following?

- Will you be able to pay your rent/mortgage this month, or next?

- Will you run out of money some time in the next three months?

- Will you be able to pay for that needed surgery when you have no medical insurance?

- Should you go to that party Saturday night when you have nothing to wear and can't afford a new outfit?

- You just got a notice that your credit card is maxed out.

- Your car needs $800 for repairs and you haven't got the money.

Remember those charming movie sirens of the 30s, 40s and 50s, where the plot had these comely ladies positioned to *catch a good man* before their wells ran dry? They were depicted coming to New York from Kansas or Iowa to find successful bachelors. These stories filled our heads with the notion that if we're cute, clever and coquettish, we, too, can be set for life. But those movies were nothing more than a wonderful escape. The reality is that it's not reality.

Before you break into a cold sweat, stop. Keep a cool head and recognize once and for all that you are your own security. It's up to you.

Several years ago there was a popular TV show, the *Golden Girls*. Four *well over 50* year old women lived together in residential suburbia for companionship as well as sharing the financial load. It was a smart concept, before its time. There are, however, many women who are adamant that they don't want roommates and need their privacy. And since moving in with our kids is not a viable option for many of us, what alternatives do we have if we don't have a plan?

**"If you are given a choice between money and sex appeal, take the money. As you get older, the money will become your sex appeal."
(Katherine Hepburn, *actress*)**

This isn't cynical; it's real. Though there may be occasional exceptions, the average man doesn't want a woman who wants him only for his money. You don't have to earn a huge salary, live in a big home or have oodles of savings. But smart money sense and practical spending is part of the package that will serve you well and make what you bring to the table more appealing. *Later in life love* can dwindle pretty fast if a woman demonstrates she is unable to manage her finances. A woman who goes through money quickly, spends frivolously, and can't save for the future will be a turn-off for most men.

There may be health issues, or children issues, or general lifestyle issues that require greater financial oversight, and a woman who *doesn't have a mind for figures* is as out-dated as the movies that promoted that stereotype. For every woman who succumbed to the notion that she shouldn't *worry her little head over that,* millions more are learning how to make ends meet. Financial gurus such as Suze Orman can be thanked for that.

Whether you are independently wealthy or just getting by, when someone catches your eye enough for you to want to bat yours, it's important to evaluate all his qualities, business and personal. There's too much at stake to do otherwise. It doesn't matter if your focus is love or money. You have to be knowledgeable and protective about both. A man can be just as irresponsible about money as love, and just as manipulative. He may be looking for a *Sugar Mama* to bail him out of debt, pay off an ex-wife, or just give him a roof over his head. He may have a lot of charm, but little money sense, and think all he needs for a nest egg is to land in your cozy nest. Don't need love so badly that you make a bad match you'll live to regret.

When you meet someone flirt-worthy, start your mental checklist and consider:

- What does he do for a living and does it support him?
- Could he support you too, if necessary?
- Is he paying child support or alimony? How much and for how long? Is there an end in sight?
- Has he ever filed for bankruptcy? When? Why?
- Does he own or rent his home?
- Does he live with his parents, his kids or an ex-girlfriend?
- Does he have sufficient money to take care of his needs?
- Does he wine and dine you like Diamond Jim Brady but live like Sloppy Joe?
- Does he complain that his wife, kids, or parents tap him for money all the time?
- Does he try to borrow money from you?

Here's a head's up: Just as you are wondering about him, that new man in your life may be thinking some of these very same questions about you! In the second half of life, the lines between romance and practicality become a little blurry. Success in all things comes from finding the right balance but there's no balance if one of you brings nothing to the equation.

Here are some of the things you don't want to happen:

- You give up alimony and marry a man who ultimately can't support you.
- You find yourself paying his financial obligations.
- You're asked to put *his* name on the deed to *your* house.
- You give up a good job for someone who leaves you and thus, no honey and no money.
- You find yourself forced to consider filing bankruptcy with your new man.
- You lose a wonderful man because he's turned off by your debts.
- You lose Mr. Terrific because he isn't looking for Ms. Needy.

You don't want to be the nurse or the purse.

That may sound cold, but sometimes it's important to slow down long enough to discover if your love object is really touched by you, or you're merely being touched on. You don't need to turn into a hardcore skeptic; just be aware and approach a new relationship with your eyes open and your wallet closed.

We interviewed a man about whether he thought most women would be receptive to taking care of men physically, financially and emotionally as they age. He responded candidly, *"If you haven't been paying the premiums, you can't expect a payback."* He was being realistic about what a man needs to do to be cared for – and about – in his mature years, especially if it's a new relationship. The same applies to women when they meet a man at this age. What do they owe you? You haven't shared high school, college, the early hard work years or children. Perhaps they don't want to be cast in the role as *provider* but you don't necessarily want the job of caregiver either. As we age, we all need to be more realistic about the give and take, pluses and minuses of older romance and the practical issues that inevitably will follow. Keeping an open mind and the ability to discuss such matters candidly (and hopefully, kindly) will go a long way to establishing trust and realism about each other's expectations.

"Love lasteth long as the money endureth."
**(William Caxton, *15th century English merchant, diplomat,*
writer and printer)**

Some practical tips to consider while you get your financial house in order:

- **Pick the right job** not solely for the pay but one where you will also be fulfilled. This provides the greatest security long term. It's easy to pick the highest paying job, but if it isn't what you enjoy, you'll be unhappy and out of work in a few months, or enduring a slow death just for a paycheck. Whether you're continuing on your career path, getting into the workforce after a long hiatus, trying to re-career into something new or just trying to slow down, look at all the aspects of a job in terms of how it can meet your life needs now. In addition to what you will earn, look at how it can satisfy your need for some flexibility, what benefits are provided and the extent of the job's, wear and tear on your body or psyche (i.e. the stress factor), and more. You don't want to be too tired for love, or too stressed to enjoy life. Find a balance. At this age you deserve it.

- **Buy one outfit** that looks wonderful on you rather than three that are good but cost two or three times more. A great outfit that makes you look and feel fantastic is worth more than a few so-so ensembles that don't show you off at your best. Clean out your closet and keep those clothes that look good on the woman you are now and tomorrow. Smart dressers know how to *buy right* and accessorize to keep an ensemble looking fresh.

- **Opt for reliability.** Your car is both freedom and transportation. It needs to be safe and reliable, not fancy. Don't be *car poor* to impress others if you can drive smart instead. Between the cost of gas and upkeep, you can either feed the tank or yourself! Practicality is the new *status symbol* and expensive cars only wow the parking attendants.

- **Avoid interest charges.** Buy what you can afford to pay for now. When you add up all the money you spend on interest, you could take a trip – and that's a good way to meet someone! Tear up those cards; especially the ones that charge 20% annual interest! And department store credit is the highest, so resist the urge. If you dig a credit hole, it is a long climb to get out, if you ever can.

- **Save some money.** The financial future you save may be your own, even if it's only to the tune of twenty dollars a month. A latte here, a latte there, it all adds up. Read a book about the basics of financial management and budgeting. It will make you smarter and less afraid and more able to ask the right questions of the right people to keep you on track.

- **Ask questions.** Is there a warranty? What does it cover? What will the insurance cost? What are the interest rates? What alternative and less expensive products can do the same thing? Is there a generic brand? Dumb is not beautiful, chic or trendy.

- **Make a budget and live by it.** If you need to have a little *mad money,* then budget for that too. There may be some sacrifices you have to make, but there are many ways women fritter away money. If you can get a handle on it, you might still be able to enjoy little luxuries that won't break the bank.

- **Learn what benefits you're entitled to** and then take advantage of them. Don't be so vain you pay full price when you could get a discount for being *over 50*. Movies, restaurants, transportation and entertainment have discounts for seniors and all you have to do is ask for them.

- **Get tax advice and financial advice where needed so you can invest and spend your money cautiously.** A good advisor can save you from making costly mistakes. Ignorance isn't bliss, and it's not attractive either. The savvier you are about the way the world of finance works, the more attractive you are to everyone! *Bag Lady phobia* is real! Don't let it happen to you.

- **Confide judiciously.** Limit the number of people in whom you confide and ask financial advice from professionals, not professional con artists. The more you familiarize yourself with the rudiments of money management, the more confident you'll be, and better you'll be able to relax and think of other fun ways to spend your time!

In case you're thinking these tips throw cold water on flirting and romance, think again. Your desirability increases with confidence and self-sufficiency. Don't be naive and gullible, or become prey or predator. Flirting is a powerful game, but it needn't (and shouldn't) be a game of chance.

Chapter 13
OF RED FLAGS AND BLACK HOLES

"Once the trust goes out of a relationship,
it's really no fun lying to 'em anymore."
George Wendt, *TV actor Norm from Cheers*

We are acutely aware of major differences we encounter when flirting, courting and sparking at this age. Sure, we know about appearance, health, history and *baggage*. Those are the obvious ones. But another important difference that comes with age is *having* money, in all its many shapes and forms.

We may have real estate investments, a hefty bank account, secure retirement income and ample stocks and bonds. We may own a company or operate a successful private business. Others may have a home and some savings. Whatever it is, it's ours and likely to be much more than we had in our 20s, 30s and 40s.

The 20 year old wonders "Does he like me or does he just want to go to bed with me?" The 30-something woman is burdened with the question, "Is he really this great or is he just trying to impress me?" The 40-plus woman asks, "Am I falling for him for the right or wrong reasons?" The 50-plus woman may think she's out of the woods, with few worries. Wrong. If you thought growing up and growing older would help put your demons to rest, unfortunately, it doesn't. The 50-plus woman of means has her own unique and very real concerns. "Is he after me for my money?"

Distrust plus romance makes for unhappy, but not uncommon, bedfellows. Think about it.

If you have assets, whether earned, inherited, or saved, it's essential that you be vigilant. Vulnerability, stupidity, and just plain being naïve can easily part a woman from her assets.

The younger set may have a bit more pep and a little less sag but they often don't yet have our acquisitions. Nor do they necessarily have estates to protect, inheritance issues, imminent old age to plan for or grown children (and maybe even grandchildren) to consider.

What's the problem? Simple. Did that 30-something guy who just lifted an eyebrow and flexed a muscle give you a million kilowatt smile because you've still got it or because of your chic Mercedes? Did that nice looking gent just brush up against you because you're looking good or because you look like a good place to park while he gets back on his feet after a financially draining divorce?

Are you being too suspicious, defensive, or insecure when you wonder if the flirtation is sincere or a stab at a perceived deep pocket? Probably not. The older we get the harder it is to recover from financial setbacks. Being cautious isn't paranoid. It's smart to watch out for your survival.

Once you get good at this flirting game, you have to think carefully about with whom you are flirting. It may be flattering and fun to have men falling at your feet. It's easy to get giddy and light headed from a sense of power and attraction but be careful. Be discriminating. Beware.

Here are some *be on the lookout tips* when you've just met a new man:

- Do his questions go beyond what you do, to what you earn?
- Are there any questions about where you bank and what's on deposit?
- Do his questions probe further than what you own to queries about cash flow?
- Has he asked about your portfolio, net worth or borrowing power?
- Has he raised the topic of money, more than once?
- Are there any questions about whether you have dependents that count on you?

If the answer to any of the above is yes, go slowly. No one should be asking these kinds of questions during the first few encounters. Flirting is fun, not business. At the beginning, attraction is chemical and we don't mean the old New York bank. You want the allure to be light and playful in those first early get-togethers. Your business, and his, needs to be revealed slowly over time, as you each become more interested, confident and trusting of one another.

It's normal to want to understand each other's financial stability but there's a right time for such revelations and the flirty first date isn't it. Take your time to learn about him before you share the intimate details of your fortune.

**"With money in your pocket, you are wise
and you are handsome and you sing well too!"
(Yiddish Proverb)**

An attractive *over 60* woman we met told us about an unnerving encounter she had when applying for some new insurance. The agent, a personable, unmarried man twenty years her junior, came to her home to go over her options. He saw a well-dressed divorcee living alone in a home filled with expensive antiques and collectible artwork. Initially polite and professional, he became flattering and personal. At the conclusion of their business, he suggested they get together for dinner. She declined.

Was she too insecure to see herself with a younger man? Not at all.

"I can easily see myself with a younger man," she explained. *"I have the energy and the interest. But I noticed he wore a tired old suit, drove a beat up car and I concluded that he was probably interested in finding a quick route to upgrading both."*

Not all flimflam flirts are so obvious. How hard is it to be charmed? It's easy to be vulnerable to the right lines and the right looks, and that's okay. Only don't put away your antennae just yet. You've heard that expression, *"there's no fool like an old fool"* but you don't have to be one. We are all susceptible to the inclination to apply blinders when there's something or someone we so very much want. It's easy and tempting to avoid seeing the flaws. It's not foolish to enjoy the flirtation, but it is foolish to succumb to the attentions of a fortune hunter who has made you his target. The price you pay can be devastating if you ignore the signs that you are being hustled.

**"Money lent to a friend must be recovered from an enemy."
(German proverb)**

The best of the conning lovers still counts on the one thing that keeps them in business – your willingness to believe because of your need for affection.

If the flirtation has led to a date and you see the conversation veering in any of the following directions, steer yourself down a different path:

1. **A loan!** Usually this is accompanied with an explanation like: *"It's just a short term cash flow set back and I'll repay you in no time at all"* or *"Just*

to tide me over until my CD matures" or *"I can't believe how late they are getting me my check. You're the first person I'll pay back when it arrives"*, and so on. Don't give the loan and don't accept another date.

2. **Business partners!** Generally you'll hear something like: *"I have the greatest idea guaranteed to make a fortune if I only had the start up capital"* or *"Everyone has climbed on board this baby, it's a sure thing. Maybe I can get you into the last offering but you have to move fast"* or *"My cousin, friend or neighbor is worth a fortune and he's going to let me come in on this investment, but I don't have the money until my (blank) matures. If you advance the money, I'll cut you in on the profit and you'll make a ton."* Gee, these all seem like swell ideas and you're sure to make a killing! Take our advice. Smile, turn your pockets inside out, walk away and kill the romance.

3. **One car payment/credit card payment/rent payment!** It starts out as just the one payment that gets your love puppy out of a jam. Then it escalates to two, three and ultimately the classic line: *"If I had known you weren't going to help out, I'd have made other arrangements, but you really led me to believe you'd be there for me!"* Try to remember what we call the *potato chip* syndrome. When was the last time anyone settled for *just one?* It's the same thing when you make one payment as a favor. When asked, try answering, *"Sorry, wrong number."*

4. **Real estate buddies!** Here's a clue how it might happen. You're snuggling, feeling warm and fuzzy all over and then the flirtatious devil has a divine idea, *"Wouldn't it be fun if we bought a little place together in Maui or Cancun or Park City or Aspen or Sri Lanka?"* Whatever! Wherever! How hard is it to work up excitement about your new romance in an exotic new place? Not very. Only listen carefully. Are the details a bit sketchy on how this *joint* purchase will be made? How about who will pay the mortgage? Have the words *insurance, taxes and association fees* even been mentioned? Or have the words *love nest, hideaway,* or *our place* been the dominant themes of the conversation? For the time being, settle for a place you can rent temporarily. It's called a hotel.

5. **Cars, clothes and cocaine!** Everyone has a weakness for something. It may start as passing conversation about a particular passion or object, such as *"How nice it would be if someone wanted to buy me a gift"* or *"Oops, guess whose birthday is coming up"* or the saga/sad story, *"My life would be complete if only..."* Too bad satisfying that passion is so expensive. If your new flame is looking for a fairy godmother to grant his wishes, let him know she only exists in fairy tales!

6. **The guilt pitch:** *"No one's ever understood me like you do"*, or *"If only I had enough money"*, or *"If you loved me you would…"* and so on. Steer clear of expensive purchases until you know the person well enough to know that your gift is appreciated and will be reciprocated. Think about whether your generosity has been prompted by just that – sincere generosity – or due to manipulation or expectation from your new interest. Gratitude can be fleeting until he extracts the next purchase, and the next. Don't fall into that trap.

Costs can be more than financial. There are the emotional tolls we pay as well, when the stakes and the mistakes are big enough. Perhaps you've heard the country western song about *"looking for love in all the wrong places"* and some of the real life tragedies about women being duped and conned. Of course, we all believe we're smarter than that and that it can't or won't happen to us. And it shouldn't, unless we allow it to by ignoring the warning signs.

There are men who will say anything to curry your favor. The emotionally eager man requires some caution, but be on the lookout for the emotionally stingy man who presents a different set of problems. Some of these *red flags* should get you thinking about what comprises a red flag for you.

You know that color when it appears, though you may foolishly put on blinders. These are moments when you've seen or heard something and it just doesn't feel right. It's those times when you have a bad feeling; when your gut knows before your head does. Don't avoid the warning signs. If we learned to trust our guts more, we could avoid a lot of heartache, betrayal, and disappointment.

Look long and hard if the man you meet is intractable on certain issues. For example:

1. **"My children always come first."** This sounds perfectly natural to say and to hear. You may even say it, too. But what this may mean is that you won't come first. Ever. Are vacations always going to be planned around (or even with) his children? Will money be shared with you or is it for only his kids? How many phone calls a day are to you and how many to his children? If you don't mind always being *second*, ignore the signals and jump into whatever space *is* made available for you.

2. **"Love me, love my dog."** As we learn to live alone, it's easy to understand the attachment to beloved pets. In fact, pets (cat, dog, horse, or iguana) may be one's primary relationship. He may want you to bond right away. If pets are your thing, great, but if not, our suggestion is to avoid forcing the issue. Just enjoy each other's company. If the pet becomes a sticking point, then you need to know where you

are in the pecking order. If you're always taking a back seat to Fido, you're barking up the wrong tree.

3.   **"Don't go there. That topic is off limits."** Ooh. You've brought up a subject that is too sensitive or he is too closed off to discuss. It doesn't really matter what the topic is, but how he reacts to being open and sharing with you may be indicative of how he will either confront or avoid other difficult conversations. Those sensitive, prickly subjects often involve such matters as health, finances, sex, past relationships, religion, family, and politics. If a relationship is to grow and become more intimate, you need to be able to explore areas that are not always easy, without fear of recrimination, argument, or dreaded silence. If you've fallen for a guy who bails when the conversation gets tough, you may have to consider if you should hang around or do your own bailing.

4.   **"I only drink/smoke/do drugs/gorge because right now I'm under a lot of stress. I'll stop eventually."** OK. When? Ever notice how excuses and promises seem to go hand in hand? The rationalization is that once everything is fine, the offending behavior (does he really believe it's offensive?) will stop because circumstances have changed. But that's not often how it works. The behavior of doing an undesirable action as a reaction to an outside stress is plain and simple weakness. Whenever things don't go his way, he'll no doubt revert to the same behavior and justifications. Life always provides stressful moments, and if the fallback position is unhealthy, that's a black hole into which you do not want to descend.

5.   **"You need a man around here."** And maybe that's true. But depending on when you hear that, it could be a red flag that turns into a black hole. It starts simply enough. First a toothbrush. Then an extra outfit or two, just in case. It seems charming and optimistic, but if it occurs after the first sleepover, take note: why is his need to curl up in your nest so strong? Does he need a home? Is his rent due soon? Is his lease up? Is he between domiciles or jobs? Is he so needy you're about to be smothered or so insecure he has to mark his turf and keep out all other contenders? There are a lot of *over-50* men who haven't managed their financial lives well, and while they may be looking for love, they may also be looking for pads where they can crash. Go slow, is our advice, and avoid the tendency to start finding closet space for him before you really get to know what he has (or will have) in the closet.

6.   **His kids give you the cold shoulder when you meet.** But you'll surely win them over, right? How could they not love you, when you

make Dad so happy? It doesn't matter that you didn't break up their happy home (assuming you didn't!). It doesn't matter that you are a great and loving gal. You're not *their* Mom. Perhaps they're suspicious of your life and your motives. Are you a gold digger? Will Dad be sharing their future inheritance with you? Will Dad's interest in you make him less available to them? Who knows? They may have their own selfish agendas and you're in the way. It's best to be patient and not press for them to like you. Let things take their course. Cautiously approach them as you would a strange dog; with fingers curled under, patiently waiting for them to sniff you out and see that you're safe. And don't underestimate this truth: blood is thicker than water. If they're interfering with your relationship, think long and hard before you let cupid pierce his arrow into your heart, and turn his back while you bleed.

7. **But I need you!** Need a project? Some women love a project, especially when their nurturing qualities have been languishing for some time. How many women have been sure they can turn a sow's ear into a silk purse? His business is failing and you can help him by working by his side. His health has been neglected and you can get him on the road to wellness. His friends have forsaken him, but you will show him what devotion means. He needs you! And doesn't that feel great? After all, that's what love is about, right? There are a lot of women who hunger to use their nurturing muscles, but no matter how deep the hunger, be discriminating. Don't mistake being needed for being in love.
    It's one thing to be there for someone you love. It's another thing to prematurely provide that level of caring before the relationship has been fully vetted.

8. **"I forgot my wallet."** Or the credit card is rejected. OK. It happens sometimes. But if it manipulates you into paying without being reimbursed, it's time to reconsider the romance. Sharing expenses from time to time isn't the issue. The problem is when you are put in the position of covering the tab when you didn't expect to do so. If you invite someone out, it's reasonable to expect you will pay. Similarly, the opposite is true. We are still old school, and some of you may object to this point of view. This is not about feminism; it's about human nature. There is still some primordial need for men to want to demonstrate they are able to *provide*, and *protect*, and paying for a date is a small way to do so. If he doesn't feel that way, start asking some questions. Why is he content to let you pay? How many times has the thought occurred to you that you would prefer a less expensive night out and

for your man to have paid? There are many other ways you can show your appreciation to even the balance sheet. You can cook him a dinner; entertain his family or business associates; help him pick out clothing or a gift; tend to him when he's sick. The list is endless. We're not advocating that you be a taker, but that you allow the man to be a giver. If he's not a giver, is he a keeper?

9. **"You're going to love when we go…"** One of the best parts of a new relationship is all the new vistas that can open in your life. What fun to have someone take you to Paris for the first time, or teach you how to snorkel or introduce you to classical music, jazz, folk dancing, Italian food, collecting seashells, and more. But there is a fine line between sharing and controlling. Is he interested in what you want to do, where you want to go, and what you want to see? Many women are swept away by the man who seems so in control. In fact, after being in charge all day, many women want to relinquish control to men and just sit back and enjoy the ride. But it can also become a problem. Are you ever going to the movie, concert, or restaurant you prefer? Does he always insist on making every decision? Is he comfortable with you making decisions at all or sulk when you try? This is a hole that's easy to fall into. Make sure you walk together and not several steps behind because if you fall into the hole, you fall alone.

Get out there, play, have a good time, but don't play stupid. Flirt, laugh, enjoy, and feel good. It's healthy and normal. But now that you're out of the shell, keep your eyes and ears open. Listen to what's said, and what's not said. If it doesn't sound right, smile and walk away. Don't waste your love (or your money!) on the wrong person, because as Sigmund Freud so pointedly stated: *"Not all men are worthy of love."*

Chapter 14
DADDY'S LITTLE GIRL

"The course of true love never did run smoothly."
William Shakespeare, *playwright*

The relationship between parents and children, especially adult children, is complicated. While we were busy growing older, our kids were growing up and the balance of power shifted to give them a greater voice in our lives.

These *mini-me* versions of ourselves can be a joy to behold. Unfortunately, they can also wreak havoc on our days and nights. We may have mellowed with age and experience (humbled by mistakes, disappointments, and life in general), but often they are full of self-righteous wisdom on how we should be living our lives, and with whom. No longer are we worried about getting our parents approval for our actions. We now need to curry the favor of our children, and they can be a lot less forgiving.

Grown children still want stability from their parents. Normalcy. Status quo. Many of them don't want you to convert their rooms into wine cellars, move to a condo or ship to them their boxes of memorabilia. Kids want things to stay the same because you are their rock, and they need for you to remain so. You should stand still while the world rotates around them. They don't want to be flexible, or rather, they don't want you to be so flexible you begin to change your life from what they have come to know. They want life to be as they want it to be, and your divorce, widowhood, or reversals of fortune rattle their comfort zones.

It's bad enough that your singlehood compromises their need for *happy family* or Kodak moments at various times and particular holidays, but when you introduce someone new into their lives, they are often a lot less welcoming than you'd like them to be. Just when you hoped they'd be the gracious children you raised, you find suspicious and hostile strangers who are guarded rather than welcoming and tough rather than warm. *"Who is this new man and what does he want with you? I don't like the way he dresses, laughs, or looks at you."* Voicing their superficial criticisms often masks the real underlying anxiety your new romance brings to your children's lives.

Our kids don't want to see us hurt, exploited, cheated, or taken. They also don't want to compete for our time with someone who might have his own ideas of how to live. They don't want their lives inconvenienced by having to incorporate your new love interest into their homes and holidays, introducing their children to someone who may or may not be permanent. Just when we're getting comfortable practicing our social skills, they seem to have forgotten their manners!

Reality shows aside, rarely are there adult sons or daughters who are eager to fix Mom or Dad up with someone new. *"You're looking for happiness? Why can't you just be content with our love? What is this about romantic love, at your age? You want to do what? Wait, don't tell us!"*

The need for love – romantic love – never dies. It changes form, but not its substance. When you introduce new elements into the lives of your children, there is often a plethora of unresolved issues that previously remained dormant, but when pressed or pinched or threatened, tend to emerge in a variety of unpleasant and even destructive ways. Both men and women have issues with grown daughters and sons who judge their choices of romantic interest. If you've made a few mistakes along the way, you can be sure those mistakes will be used against you to undermine your confidence in your ability to choose wisely. If you weren't smart before, what's so different now? If a man has been monogamous for 35 years to the same woman his children knew and loved as Mom, how could he find someone else attractive? *Especially that tramp!*

Rather than get upset when your adult children become protective, anticipate making the necessary adjustments and be sensitive as to how and when you introduce your new *friend* into their lives. Do it right, and they may grow to accept this person. Do it wrong and you risk alienating them or abandoning your prospects for a loving partner and a relationship with someone your own age.

This rivalry is new territory and it's important to understand where the boundaries and potholes are if you want a chance at being more than just an on-call babysitter or a deep pocket for your kids. Carving out the time (and the right) to have a loving relationship with someone is something that takes fortitude and courage to address, and if you approach it with your eyes open, you can prepare yourself and your children for what may come your way.

If you and your partner deal with it together, it will make you allies as well as making it less likely that the grown kids can drive a wedge between you. There is strength in numbers!

Whether you move forward and become a family, or remain lovers or friends, you want your time together to be enjoyable, without the fear of threats and reprisals from the kids. How bad can it be?

Consider some of these war stories from the *front*:

- Caryn received text messages threatening death from her fiancé's younger son. She had to get a restraining order against him.

- Shelly's daughter went off to college, but refused to come home for Christmas dinner if *"that guy was going to be there"*.

- John's daughters did an intervention one Sunday morning, insisting that he stop seeing *that woman* until *they* were ready for him to date again.

- Colleen's son refused to let her visit the grandchildren unless she came alone.

- Jack attended his mother's funeral with his girlfriend Claire. At the graveside, his son came over to pointedly tell Claire she wasn't welcome at the post-funeral reception reserved for friends and family.

- Carl's daughter threatened to drop out of college if he didn't stop dating.

- Lynn's grown son chastised her for smiling when her new man complimented her appearance in front of her kids. *"What kind of a man makes remarks like that, at your age!"*

The cruelty of grown children can be devastating, and many relationships never get beyond it. Is it easier to succumb to the kids and give up on love, than to try and get them to understand your wish for romantic love? Sure. It's always easier to give up, but don't, if you want a life of your own.

If you've been widowed, your children will have their own timetables for when, or if, you can resume having a social life. They will want to set the terms, the criteria, and may even believe they have the right as well as the obligation to choose your mate, if they deem it suitable for you to have one. And for some, that's a big if.

If you've been divorced, the attitude may be even more critical towards you and your efforts. After all, you failed before and they already have a Dad. Often the biggest obstacle is getting adult children to understand that it's not about them. It's about you.

Here are some suggestions that can make it easier for you during this time:

1. **Don't assume you can talk to your kids about everything.** Even though they are adults and you want to be friends, talking about your romantic life is not going to be easy for them. As much as you want to include them in adult conversations, with adult topics, when it comes to your relationships, perhaps the less they know the better. You're still their *Mom*.

2. **Don't ask their advice about personal matters.** They don't want to be your confidante. They can help you pick a tax shelter, a car, or set your VCR to the right time, but serving as your advisor in affairs of the heart is not in their job description.

3. **Don't take them into your confidence about the private moments you share with your dates.** About this, they *really* don't want to know!

4. **Don't give them advice about their love lives, now that your social life is on the upswing.** Well-meaning as your comments might be, they may resent your unsolicited opinions as intrusive and see that as an invitation to contribute their two cents to your romantic life. So let's call this a standoff and remember, you're in a learning curve too!

5. **Don't insist that every family event include your new someone.** It may take time for your kids to get acclimated to the idea that you are not always going to be alone. Ease them into it and don't draw a line in the sand that says, *"Love me, love my boyfriend"*. It may take a while.

6. **Don't stop dating because your kids feel weird about it.** That's their problem, not yours. They will adjust to your having a social life in time. Don't succumb to their intimidation: *"We don't want you bringing your boyfriend over and confusing our kids. He's not going to be their grandpa. We don't feel comfortable with a parade of men in and out of our lives."* In spite of the fact that they say they're only looking out for your happiness, in truth, they are possibly being more selfish than even they realize. Go on with your life and see them when you can.

7. **Don't cry on their shoulders.** If you break a hip, they will be there for you. If your heart is broken, you're on your own. If you are unhappy, it isn't fair to expect them to lift you out of your funk. For better or worse, you're in this alone. Cultivate a good friend for this job and these confidences.

8. **Don't stop having private time with your children and grandchildren, even though you may need to set some boundaries on your availability.** They need to know they still matter to you, and

that they aren't losing your love or your attention because you have someone new to care about. If you show them less interest, they will be jealous of your time, and the person with whom you are spending it.

"Jealousy is the tie that binds, and binds, and binds."
(Helen Rowland, *writer*)

Aside from the normal reactions of your adult children to your newfound desire to date, there are some warning signs to heed that may serve as a precursor to some of the more challenging moments you could face in dealing with his children.

The *other* other woman...

"When they said *'hell hath no fury like a woman scorned'* I had no idea they were referring to my date's adult daughter," Gretchen tearfully cried as she sank forlornly into an armchair! Her story was similar to others we'd heard and boiled down to the same bottom line: an adult daughter's sabotage of her Dad's new love.

Let's face it, in romance, the prospect of the other or younger woman is always there. But there's another more unexpected source of competition that can be more challenging: *Daddy's Little Girl*.

With accusations ranging from manipulator to *"where'd you find that bitch!"* the jibes are intended to divide and conquer any hope of happiness between you and Dad.

Gretchen's plight is not unique, nor is the experience of being out together, when, uh oh...there goes the cell phone. *"Gotta take this,"* he muffles. *"It's my daughter."*

Some older men haven't figured out that their loving daughters seem to be calling more often during dinner, late at night, or when they know Dad has plans. Are they suddenly more solicitous of his well-being or needier of his attention? Do they seem to have more problems or are they just less able to handle them? Or, are their motives considerably more insidious?

Do *Daddy's Girls* love Daddy all that much more when there's a little competition?

Gretchen's Story

"Two nights ago I heard him tell Daughter #1 we were going out to celebrate our three-month anniversary. I thought it was so sweet of him to think to mention it to her. Just as we settled into the booth, he leaned over to say something I expected would be incredibly charming, but, his cell phone rang to the tune of Vivaldi's Four Seasons. It may as well have been 'Breaking Up is Hard to Do'!

Instead of finishing what he started, he pulled out the phone, looked at the caller ID and mumbled, "Daughter #1 just checking in!" and turned his head to take the call.

What's a gal like Gretchen to do? Tell him to hang up on his baby girl? Suggest he shut off the phone during dinner? Say that his daughter is an interfering, nasty piece of work? Ummm… that would be no, no and NO!

"But there's more," Gretchen continued. "Once he hung up I hoped we could recapture the moment. But, as he raised his glass again in a toast, there went Vivaldi with Daughter #2 weighing in. That was no coincidence. I know they're determined to break us up. I just know it. When is it going to be my season?"

What accounts for such deliberate sabotage? A man's adult daughters may fear any or all of the following:

1. You're after Dad for his money.

2. You'll distract Dad from them and their families.

3. You'll get your hands on their inheritance.

4. You'll turn Dad against them.

5. You'll expect Dad to spend time with your family and not theirs.

6. You'll be more important to Dad than they are.

7. You'll make their Mom feel jealous or sad if Dad is divorced.

8. You'll try to convince the world that Dad loves you more than his late wife.

Looking out for Dad's interests, as well as their own, is the job of daughters. They aren't all out to do you in, but they do want to be certain if you're doing Dad, that you're doing no wrong – to him or to them.

Family law attorneys frequently hear from adult children when they sense a new relationship may be getting serious. Suddenly Dad's kids strive to become experts in the area of prenuptial agreements, followed by calls to the estate-planning attorney asking such questions as *"can we be cut out of the will?"* In the early stages of dating, this kind of interference is easier to ignore. But don't ignore it forever. It may signal a future problem likely to rear its ugly head later on. Like the most toxic substance, adult children can spread a poison that kills all in its path.

Malicious chatter disguised as well-intentioned suggestions can be the beginning of the end for Gretchen, or for you. Sure, not all men are going to be susceptible to their children's nasty innuendos but the reality is that once it starts, it can take on a life of its own. It's a bad idea to try to convince your man that his children are the villains because most likely you're going to lose if he has to choose between you and his family.

It's also a bad idea to try to win the girls over by being overly friendly, solicitous and too giving. They'll see through it, no matter how sincere you are, and re-double their efforts to loosen your grip on their Dad. The wiser course is to maintain a watchful and respectful distance. Know that their relationship is paramount and if you choose to accept that, eventually they may come around to accepting you. Try to shift the balance of power to you and you'll see your power erode.

If daughters are determined to think the worst of you (assuming no justification for such thoughts) it's unlikely you'll be able to do anything to dissuade them. Only time and experience can do that. But sometimes, if you're very, very good, you might be able to soften the ice, if not outright break it.

But what about how son's react to the *other* man?

Sons can be wonderful and they can be tyrants. They often see themselves in the role of caretaker, coming over to fix what's broken (if they can) or arrange to have it done. They'll drive you places and drive you crazy. We adore them (most of the time) but they can be terribly overbearing when they see that a new man is sniffing around.

Adult sons are protective, and suspicious. If Mom has resources, they don't want to see them exploited by some fortune hunter. If Mom is emotionally vulnerable, they don't want to see her heart broken.

Adult sons can be terribly judgmental and even menacing toward Mom's suitors, willing to drive them away before the first ding-dong doorbell rings. Initially their overprotective zeal may seem cute but that can wear thin. After a while, as the choices get slimmer and the lonely nights lonelier, their overbearing protectiveness may interfere and even destroy the possibility for love.

Some things to consider to keep sons and daughters calm through the dating process include:

- **Don't talk to them about your romantic feelings or sexual attraction.** Never the best information to share with the kids! They don't want to know. Trust us.

- **Don't flirt in front of them.** It makes them uncomfortable to see you in the role of seductress. It's not a side of you they want to know.

- **Don't expect them to like your new beau just because you do.** Give them time to see you in a new light, and him in the light of day.

- **Don't impose your new guy on them or their families.** Ask if he can be included and graciously accept their answer, even if it's no. Don't force the issue by insisting your date come along. Keep the lines of communication open, and gently keep asking the next time.

- **Don't allow your fellow to make suggestive remarks about you in their presence.** Your child will see such talk as disrespect rather than desire. Remember, they think they have exclusivity on romance – not old Mom.

"In dreams and in love there are no impossibilities." (Janus Arany, *journalist, writer, poet*)

Some families blend well. It's not an impossibility. Some families, if not blended, are at least lightly folded together. It can happen. But it takes a concerted effort to start off on the right foot and smart maneuvering to make sure not to step on so many toes!

When finally introduced to your love's adult children, it is helpful to convey, at the right time, the following:

1. You're not trying to displace, replace or compete with their Mom or with them.
2. You have your own money and assets.
3. You will welcome them to your family events.
4. You respect their private time with Dad.
5. You're not trying to be their Mom, just a friend.
6. You are not in competition with them for their Dad's affection.
7. You know they come first.

Of course, there is the possibility of some pleasant surprises. Adult children may be delighted to have you on the scene if you have more economic clout than Dad, or if Dad is physically in decline and they welcome having someone to take good care of him. Perhaps Dad has been too involved in their lives because he didn't have one of his own. Then it's a different story. Or, they just may be happy that Dad is happy and welcome you with open arms!

Chapter 15
ONCE YOU HAVE FOUND HIM, NEVER LET HIM GO?

"Life is so constructed that an event does not, cannot,
will not match the expectation."
Charlotte Bronte, *author*

You've excelled in flirting and mastered dating. What could go wrong? Or better said, what if things go right? Are you ready for the next step and what that means? Is it possible to be less ready in our middle years than we were in our 20s?

It is almost an absolute certainty that adult children, both yours and his, will be asking a lot of questions if love has knocked on your door. This is something that requires a deep breath and some pause for thought. There is a big difference between marriage and dating, and do not for one minute, think that all the children from both sides (maybe even grandchildren, too!) will not factor into your consideration.

Do you want to take the next step?

Assuming you do, what about *I do?*

Have you thought about how you'd react if things actually got to the proposal stage? What about the specter of a pre-nuptial agreement? Do you need estate planning to protect you financially if you remarry? If remarriage entails giving up existing alimony from a previous marriage, can you afford to take that risk? Do you have the right to demand certain conditions from your intended to protect your interests? Is it unreasonable to ask if he has life insurance or if you will be included as a beneficiary in his estate?

These questions (and many more) will undoubtedly raise eyebrows for both your and his adult children. They need to be addressed at the right time and in the right way. If you are discovering there is no right time or right way, he may not be the right man for you.

> **"Before you attempt to beat the odds,**
> **be sure you could survive the odds beating you."**
> **(Larry Kersten, *sociologist, author*)**

Elizabeth's Story

Elizabeth, a successful realtor, was in love with David and had become close with his grown family. She couldn't do enough for them, personally or professionally. When David's son and daughter-in-law needed a house, Elizabeth invested months helping them find the perfect home, only to accidentally discover later that they had opened escrow through another agent without ever telling her. Betrayed and angry, she accused David's family of being selfish, arrogant, and thoughtless. She no longer wanted to see his family, only David, whom she still loved and expected would take her side.

She believed that his love for her would trump his devotion to his kids. Big mistake! While she might have been right about the merits of the situation, she was wrong in assuming that being right was good enough.

First, David avoided the subject altogether. Then holidays came and Elizabeth realized she wasn't invited to the family gatherings, and more importantly, that David had chosen to spend the holidays with his kids and without her. Of course, the inevitable happened and David, kindly but definitively, broke it off.

What went wrong?

- Elizabeth caused a showdown between her and his kids, and lost, as women usually will.

- Elizabeth tried too hard and ultimately felt used and exploited, since her expectations for reciprocal affection weren't met.

- Elizabeth overestimated her power and underestimated theirs, by thinking that new love could eclipse the old love of children and parents.

- Elizabeth naively presumed she had earned an unshakable seat at the family table.

> **"Sometimes you have to get to know someone really well**
> **to realize you're really strangers."**
> **(Mary Tyler Moore, *actress on The Mary Tyler Show*)**

If you are happy and things are going well, enjoy yourself but never become too complacent. Don't confuse confidence and cockiness. Don't confuse attitude and arrogance. No matter how deep feelings run, your new partner has a past and history and if there are children, they will play a role. What that role is varies from partner to partner, but failing to understand the role is a mistake. If this is the man for you, figure out how to fold the rest of his life into your life, together. If you don't, you could have an ending or a soap opera.

The reality is, if the kids dislike, suspect, or barely tolerate you, why would you want to hold on to this man? At our age, a sound relationship requires a lot of give and take. If your guy has adult children holding him back, you're going to find yourself on the receiving end of a lot more, and a lot less, than you bargained for.

Later in life it will matter if your family, and his, have been supportive and embraced your love. As we age, we want family and friends to be with us, and for us, as we face life's challenges. Alienating their affections poisons the well in many destructive ways. It's worth working on, if you can. And if you can't, as an old Yiddish proverb states, *"You don't put a well head in a sick bed"*.

Chapter 16
NOW THAT YOU'VE CAUGHT HIM, HOW DO YOU LET HIM GO?

"You have to kiss a lot of frogs before you meet the magic prince."
Anonymous

It happens. You cast your line and the fish start jumping. Sometimes they're just what you want, and sometimes you awaken to the fact that the fish you've caught were not exactly what you were angling for. So what do you do?

Cutting one's losses and saying goodbye is rarely easy. We know how it feels to be rejected, so take pains to be gentle. But the cleanest cut heals fastest. When it's time to move on, do it face to face (preferably in a public place), and be clear. None of this, *"I'm so confused,"* nonsense. Or worse, *"It's not you, it's me,"* business. If it's not right, it's not right. You do him a disservice to pretend otherwise.

However you say *adios*, you should do it as a lady. Avoid post-it notes, emails or *Dear John* letters. How you handle difficult situations shows much about your character, and you never know when you might run into him again. Don't you want to be remembered fondly?

Joy's Story

Joy was dating a few different men, including Jake. She enjoyed his company, along with the others, but the more she got to know Jake, the more she realized he didn't have his life in order. His business deals were in flux, he was still playing out the tragedy of an ex-wife, and his car was perpetually in the shop. It always seemed to be something.

One evening, Jake called to tell her that he felt badly he couldn't take her out more often, and court her the way he would like. After this preamble, she expected the conversation to end with a mutually agreed upon goodbye. Imagine her surprise when he dropped the bomb that he was falling in love and wanted to spend the rest of his life with her. He acknowledged the timing was bad. She agreed, and told him she valued his friendship. The cool head of her reality was waking up.

Joy worried she had appeared cavalier or worse, as someone who left a man when the chips were down. For 24-hours, a noisy debate in her head plagued her waking moments: How does one reject another without being patronizing, pitying, or cruel?

The following night when they got together, the air was thick with his previous night's disclosure, and her chilly response. Joy wondered what Jake was thinking. Jake wondered what Joy had thought. Neither could relax. He regretted having said anything, and she was spooked by an intensity she didn't return. Instead of their lovemaking being the fun, exploratory experience of previous nights, Jake was performing only to prove himself and failed to notice Joy's perfunctory response. The following morning, she made fresh coffee, brought in the paper, and said: "Jake, what you shared with me the other night was loving and generous. And it made me think about the implications for us going forward. We're just in different places and I'm not anywhere close to thinking in terms of permanence, exclusivity or commitment. It would be unfair of me to pretend otherwise."

Was Jake disappointed? Yes. But devastated? No. Joy handled the situation with tact, kindness and honesty. She didn't say she was *confused, needed more time to think* or that she was *too wounded by previous relationships to commit*. She didn't fault Jake for his failures. She acknowledged him for the courage it took to declare himself, and that he deserved to be treated with respect and not be misled that her feelings for him were more than they were.

She elected to deal with Jake directly and clearly without addressing his shortcomings. She gave him credit where due, explained her own misgivings about her situation and allowed them to both exit with dignity. They remain friends to this day.

Joy is a grown-up and as such, was not interested in playing games. But she wasn't always so clear and objective. She had the benefit of learning how to graciously exit a relationship from someone who showed her the way as he showed her the door.

Before Joy met Jake, she had briefly dated Sam, a recent widower. After six years watching his wife of 35 years slowly decline from cancer, Sam's friends and family felt it was time for him to rejoin the social world. Everyone got into the act to fix him up. Joy knew that Sam was dating other women. Though she kept things light, she discovered that Sam was a man she could grow to love, given the right circumstances. She decided to see if she could take things a step further and planned a Valentine's Day surprise for him. Just before the holiday, Sam invited her to breakfast. When she walked into his house, she smiled and told him she had planned a Valentine surprise.

"Wait," he said soberly. "First read this." He handed her an envelope, which, she presumed, was a Valentine. While they stood in his foyer, she read his letter:

"Dear Joy,

I wanted to say this to you but I had to write it because I was sure I would forget something or goof it up.

Judith Scott and I have developed a very special relationship. I am very fond of her and want to spend more time with her. She has found a special place in my heart.

This relationship between Judith and me has blossomed in the past few weeks. Where it will lead to I don't know but for now, because of this, my social calendar is on hold.

I want you to know that I think you are a wonderful woman and I've enjoyed our time together. I value your friendship. This is a new experience for me to have a woman as a friend. I hope you understand and that we will remain good friends.

Sam"

Was she deflated? Perhaps. The "Valentine surprise" she had planned for Sam disappeared like smoke in the air. But she appreciated the kind, direct, uncomplicated way Sam handled this. It was clear, respectful, and done with consideration for her. There was no ambiguity, no pretense, and no games. Because he was forthright and a gentleman, they were able to remain good friends.

"Fish or cut bait."
(American proverb)

Breakups don't always go so easily. Nobody likes being rejected, particularly at this stage in life. We've all experienced loss. Now we want things to work. But there are no guarantees. How you say goodbye and how someone says goodbye to you makes all the difference in how we respond to future hellos. The hysterical crash and burn and abuse that often accompanies youthful breakups aren't ideal at any age, and certainly not for the over 50 crowd. If nothing else, we need to preserve a little dignity!

Marilyn's story…

While online, Marilyn met an intelligent, articulate, and financially secure attorney. He had been a successful litigator and was now retired. They met for coffee and he fell for her with a thud! She was everything he'd ever wanted in a woman. He wanted nothing more than to take care of her forever. One glitch. Marilyn wasn't romantically interested in him. On each date she made it clear that she liked talking with him and going to an occasional movie, but romance? Not for her, and not with him.

"Tell me why," he implored? "I can change! You make me want to be exceptional!" It was a flattering plea but maybe Marilyn should have taken heed. It can be foolish and harmful to casually date a man whose heart is so desperate for commitment. Marilyn's suitor kept pushing, making each encounter a peevish challenge instead of the fun, lively evenings of their earlier get-togethers. His obsession to be the man she wanted him to be (which was all in his head, not hers) drove him to brood about her and build a festering anger when his plan didn't work. His attempts to 'will' her to love him bordered on pathology and Marilyn rightly backed away.

Then she started receiving hang-ups on her phone at odd hours. Marilyn's friends thought she was being paranoid when she told them she felt she was being watched. Three weeks after ending their friendship, Marilyn discovered she was, and filed for a restraining order!

Marilyn didn't want to be unkind. And she didn't want to come across as unappreciative of his feelings. Her confusion and failure to accurately interpret his actions early on made it more difficult when she knew that she had to end it.

Her stalker, the former lawyer, represented himself in court and denied his actions. Perhaps the judge saw the vicious glare he gave Marilyn or perhaps he just believed her, but she was granted a restraining order to keep him away from her for three years.

Marilyn made a number of mistakes that could have been avoided if she had known how to read the signs.

Look out for:

- **A man who falls in love too fast or too easily.** As wonderful as you are, no one should have a fantasy about you too quickly and with so little information. You want to take time to build awareness and trust before you fall in love. If he falls in love too quickly, the chances are he has fallen in love with something or someone other than you. This is a recipe for disaster.

- **A man who doesn't understand the meaning of *no*.** Oh, yes, we love the idea of being pursued against all odds. It works in the movies and romance novels, but in real life – and at our age – that kind of relentless obsession is not healthy. Hearts can be hot, but we need to keep a cool head lest we get burned. When you say *no* (and mean it!) make sure you're with a man who accepts that answer.

- **Aggressive and antagonistic behavior is not passion.** Such intense feelings, just like a country music song are just that – intense! Don't confuse passion and unhealthy intensity. Is deep and unbridled love indicative of more serious and disturbing behavior? High drama may even be dangerous.

- **If you think it's stalking, it probably is.** Never hesitate to call the police or get a restraining order if you need help. You've lived long enough to know the difference between a stalker and a suitor and if your efforts to bring it to a conclusion don't work, get the assistance you need from outside sources.

- **He zigs when you zag.** If there is a major discrepancy between what he feels and what you feel, don't continue the relationship unless you both commit to the same terms and conditions.

Final words on final words: Say goodbye when you know it's not going to go any further.

Don't send mixed messages and fake reality – yours or his. Don't flatter him, seduce him, make excuses for your decision or fix a *final supper* when you say goodbye. Don't pretend that you're confused, need a little time, or want to go slow. When you pretend, *"It's my inability to love…"* you leave the door open. If you want to wash this man right out of your hair, start scrubbing.

And don't, for your sake and his, succumb to *goodbye* intimacy. Sex isn't your little going away present or just a little something to remember you by. If you allow him to pull that, *"I'm going to love you like nobody's loved you"* routine, not only will you feel worse in the morning, but you'll need a crowbar to get him out of your life.

When it's time to end it, do so with clarity and precision. Be clear. Be kind. And be gone.

Chapter 17
FLIRTING FIRE STARTERS (OR ICE BREAKERS)

"It was the best of times, it was the worst of times."
Charles Dickens, *author*

So now you get it: your potential, your need for love, and why you, too, can have it all. You've seen why and how to go about finding romance. You know a little about when and where to fish or cut bait. Moving forward, armed with motivation and confidence, perhaps you're ready for some ideas on how to get some sparks flying in your direction.

A great opening line is never forgotten, but so hard to compose. Could you use some help? Don't know where to start? Can't think of a thing to say to a stranger?

In certain safe contexts, good opening lines come more naturally. It helps when someone has a dog or a child in tow, or when you're one of a group waiting in line at the Deli. And how about when you're stuck in the airport because a flight was cancelled! You find ways to strike up a conversation when you're not thinking about it, which is the point. When you're at ease the words will find their way.

It doesn't matter if you're at a crowded party, buying cereal at the supermarket or settling into your seat at a movie. If an interesting person is within reach, it's a great opportunity and you don't want to be fumbling for words. The first words you utter can form a memorable and favorable first impression, and be the perfect icebreaker. No pressure, right? But everyone is different and the words that work for the busy executive aren't necessarily right for the reticent widower and the style of a flamboyant divorcee may not be the spirit of a more reserved homemaker.

Great lines, first impressions, ice breakers. Sometimes finding just the right words can set the tone for magic and a flicker of possibility. But there's no *one size fits all* comment that will open the door. A busy executive may have no time for small talk while a widower may have all the time in the world. There's no crystal ball telling us what lines will work, but when we asked around, we got lots of input – from the outrageous to the safe.

"If love is the answer, what is the question?"
(Lily Tomlin)

Our words set a tone and may even create a spark. Don't let an opportunity pass because you're tongue-tied. From the crazy to safe, playful to serious, we encourage you to say *something*. Perhaps one of the following lines will ignite some possibilities for you.

For the More Confident Woman Who Warms to the Warmer Approach

1. "You have a kind face."
2. "You look like the sort of guy it'd be fun to cook for."
3. "A good listener is rare and special."
4. "Your voice reminds me of a wonderful 1940s movie."
5. "You remind me of good times I've had."
6. "If I turn around and walk away right now, you may miss the adventure of a lifetime."
7. "There are a dozen good reasons why I shouldn't be starting this conversation, but when I saw you I thought of a dozen good reasons why I should."
8. "I hope you don't think I'm forward when I say I'd like to get to know you."
9. "I'm having a good hair day. Want to have lunch?"
10. "For the most part I don't have much use for men, but you look like you might be an exception."
11. "I need to buy a power drill. Which one would you suggest?"
12. "It looks like rain. Do you have an umbrella or an apartment?"
13. "I rarely find anyone interesting. You're a welcome exception. Keep talking."
14. "You look like leading man material."
15. "Hello gorgeous!"

16. "I wanted to see if you look as good close up as you did from across the room and you do."

17. "I've been searching all day for someone I'd like to take me to Paris for lunch."

18. "Let's run away together and see how it works out."

19. "If I promise not to bore you, would you buy me a drink?"

20. "If you were ice cream, I'd bet you'd be my favorite flavor."

21. "My heart's easily bruised. Be gentle."

22. "You hold my attention."

23. "The second I saw you I thought, *there is a God.*"

24. "Everyone has been trying to fix me up and then I saw you and thought maybe I could do this better on my own."

25. "You have a dazzling smile."

26. "I suppose everyone tells you that you've got great eyes. Just add me to the list."

27. "My kids tell me I need to get out more often. Who would have guessed how right my kids could be!"

28. "Nice car."

For the More Traditional (play it safe) Woman

1. "I'd love to find a good book to read this summer. Any recommendations?"

2. "I'm always getting lost. Could you point me in the right direction?"

3. "Can you recommend the best place to get my car repaired?"

4. "What's the difference between a mutual fund and a hedge fund?"

5. "Do you think real estate prices have topped out?"

6. "Are you through with the sports section of the paper?"

7. "Is that your dog? What kind is it?"

8. "Have you ever "day traded"?"

9. "How 'bout those Lakers?"

10. "I've never been in this store before. Do you know where they hide the beer?"

11. "Have you seen this movie? Would you recommend it?"

12. "My office is having a party and I've been asked to bring a casserole. Do people still eat casseroles?"

13. "I've killed all my plants. Do you have a green thumb?"

14. "My grandson is coming to visit. Any suggestions for activities?"

15. "Is this color good on me? I'm color blind."

16. "Can I borrow your cell phone for a moment?"

For the Woman Who Finds Safety in Humor

1. "You're standing on my foot."

2. "I don't have a lot of time, but I'm willing to find some for you."

3. "Do you speak English?"

4. "You're nothing like my ex-husband. We're off to a good start."

5. "Would you like to see if we could beat the odds?"

6. "It's been a long, hot summer. Care for a nice, cool drink?"

7. "I'll show you mine if you show me yours. Grandchildren pictures, that is!"

8. "I've gotten really good at making martinis. Can I shake things up for you sometime?"

9. "Aren't you that cute guy from *Sex and the City?*"

10. "Don't be so formal. We're all part of this great big mess together. Now, what did you say your name is?"

11. "I love a man with a big desk."

12. "What's the difference between rugby and football?"

13. "Do you accept business cards, scraps of paper or would you be willing to just memorize my number?"

14. "Don't tell me your name – let me guess."

15. "Aren't you that cute guy from *Law and Order?*"

16. "Could you make a list of everything you like so I do nothing wrong?"

For the Woman With Lust in Her Heart

1. "Take me home, tuck me in and we can discuss the rest."

2. "Walk away now unless you want to put an end to this dull evening."

3. "Fantastic, fabulous, ferocious. Get the picture?"

4. "So, is the rest of the package as good as what I'm seeing."

5. "Know any bedtime stories?"

6. "Can you dance or do you just look like you've got rhythm?"

7. "I'm not just a pretty face. I can cook, too."

8. "I'm looking at you and I'm thinking everything's coming up roses, you know what I mean?"

9. "You look like a guy who knows what to do."

10. "I'd say we look like a perfect fit."

11. "I'll bark, if you'll howl."

12. "My place, your place, anyplace?"

13. "I could give up celibacy for a man like you."

14. "I'm not just good looking. I know which end of the hammer to hold, too!"

15. "Great shoes."

16. "Great tie."

17. "What I lack in originality I make up in sincerity."

18. "My plans got cancelled for this evening. Want to have dinner?"

19. "Have you been here before?"

20. "You have beautiful eyes."

21. "If I had crystal ball, I think it would show my luck is changing."

Take out a pen and start writing some good lines that might work for you. Borrow some from the list above. Steal from a book, a magazine, or a song. Use a line you heard in the market, in the office, on the bus. But don't ever say that an opportunity was missed because you couldn't think of what to say. The truth is, even if your opening lines fall flat, you can recover with, *"I may stink at an opening line, but I really wanted to meet you."* Who would find that offensive? Your goal is to get a conversation going. Don't forget, most everyone has a touch of shyness and insecurity. The cure? A friendly opening line. It's a rare person who would be offended by someone showing interest.

In times of desperation, grab a line from a movie. The line from *Jerry McGuire* is a winner: *"You had me at hello."* Or consider how the country responded to the cornball guy from the movie, *The Wedding Crasher* when he said, *"Scientists say we use only 10% of our brains, but I think we use only 10% of our hearts."*

OK. It's unlikely we are going to be so creative, but whether you leave him swooning or laughing you'll at least have him curious about you, and flattered you took the time to start a conversation.

That's all flirting is: an opening, a signal, an overture. It says, *"I'm interested."* It's not a commitment. It's not forever after. It's a peek and a wink. It's the opening credits and if you and he like what follows, you may stick around and watch the story unfold and still be together when the screen fades to black.

EPILOGUE

We wrote this book to share some thoughts about the art of flirting, particularly for those who think themselves too old to be considered serious dating material. We wondered why some women always have a man in their lives, and others never do. We thought about all the times we've sat with women and heard the same concerns expressed over and over. With few exceptions the complaints stay the same and so does the behavior of the women. It is to those women who are the exceptions, successful in dating, in flirting, in meeting great guys that we owe a debt of gratitude for sharing their stories, attitudes and *techniques*.

Ladies, we're here to affirm that good men are out there – good, mature men who want good, mature women in their lives. But it takes courage to find them. It's easier, but lonelier, to just give up. Many do. But many don't, and they are the ones who are having the best of times.

You can too. It's a choice. Companionship and romance is available, but you have to expend some effort – conscious, deliberate, openhearted effort – to obtain it. Why can't you be one of those who is enjoys the balance of the journey with someone at your side? It's up to you.

"Age does not protect you from love, but love to some extent protects you from age." (Jeanne Moreau, *actress*)

About the Authors

Barbara Bellman:

Now living and loving in Washington DC, Barbara Bellman has spent her entire marketing career (30-plus years) developing strategies to put companies, products and services in the places of most potential. Understanding the female market has been a fascinating, and unexpected opportunity to learn about women from both a personal and professional perspective. As a brand strategist she has written and lectured about marketing to women, learning how to reach, motivate, inspire, persuade, educate, and change behaviors.

Barbara is the author of two books on marketing to women: *Reaching Women, The Way To Go In Marketing Health Services;* and *Hitting The Right Nerve.*

Susan Goldstein:

Susan Goldstein has practiced family law in Los Angeles, California for more than 28 years. She has represented hundreds of women, protecting their rights and counseling them about what lies ahead, as they go through the life changing experience of divorce. After speaking with and hearing the stories of women about to re-enter the singles world, Susan has a unique perspective about the fears, insecurities, anger, concerns, and frustrations that surface after divorce. She has served as both a cheerleader and coach for women as they venture back into the singles scene.

Susan is co-author of *The Smart Divorce*, a book designed to bring reason, humor and sanity to the emotional and financial minefield of divorce.

Printed in the United States
126504LV00004B/166-207/P

9 780595 428281